Psychology AS

The Mini Companion

Cara Flanagan

Published in 2003 by:
Nelson Thornes Ltd
Delta Place
27 Bath Road
CHELTENHAM
GL53 7TH
United Kingdom

03 04 05 06 07 / 10 9 8 7 6 5 4 3 2 1

A catalogue record for this book is available from the British Library.

ISBN 0 7487 7543 9

Page make-up by GreenGate Publishing Services, Tonbridge

Printed and bound in Spain by GraphyCems

Contents

This book is a mini version of *Psychology AS: The Complete Companion*. It contains just the basic information needed for the AQA specification A AS examination. There are no frills and no extras.

When a cook makes a special sauce he or she will boil the liquid for a long time so that it reduces in volume leaving just the most essential (and tasty) ingredients. That's what I have done here – producing the nuggets of knowledge necessary to enable you to focus on what you *must* learn as distinct from what you *could* learn in order to do well in the exam. In order to *understand* some of the information presented here you will need to read other books, such as the *Complete Companion*.

The book is organised as follows:

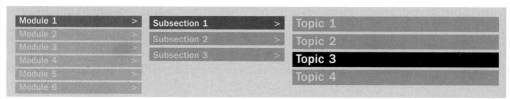

The AQA specification A AS consists of 6 modules (or sections) (cognitive psychology, developmental psychology, physiological psychology, individual differences, social psychology and research methods).

Each module is subdivided into three subsections.

In this book topics have been identified within each subsection. Each topic is covered on a *single page*.

In total there are a mere 48 topics plus research methods (covered on 6 pages)!

The book starts with some details about the examination and tips for doing well in the final examination.

There are three unit exams.

Each unit contains two sections.

Unit 1: Cognitive Psychology and Developmental Psychology

Each of the unit exams is one hour in duration.

Unit 2: Physiological Psychology and Individual Differences

Unit 3: Social Psychology and Research Methods

You have to answer **two** questions in one hour, selecting one question from each section (and there are two questions in each section).

Research methods is different (it will be described later).

This is what an exam paper looks like

SECTION A – Cognitive Psychology

Answer **one** question from this Section.

You should attempt all parts of the question you choose.

---

1   Total for this question: *30 marks*

(a) Describe **three** differences between short-term memory and long-term memory.
(2 marks + 2 marks + 2 marks)

(b) Outline findings of research into duration in long-term memory. *(6 marks)*

(c) Outline and evaluate the multi-store model of memory. *(18 marks)*

2   Total for this question: *30 marks*

(a) Describe **two** explanations for forgetting in short-term memory. *(3 marks + 3 marks)*

(b) Describe the procedures and findings of **one** study of flashbulb memories. *(6 marks)*

(c) 'Eyewitness testimony is extremely unreliable.'
Consider psychological research into eyewitness testimony. *(18 marks)*

SECTION B – Developmental Psychology

Answer **one** question from this Section.

You should attempt all parts of the question you choose.

---

1   Total for this question: **30 marks**

(a) What is meant by secure and insecure attachments? *(3 marks + 3 marks)*

(b) Outline Bowlby's maternal deprivation hypothesis. *(6 marks)*

(c) Assess the extent to which research (theories **and/or** studies) support the view that day care has negative effects on children's cognitive development *(18 marks)*

2   Total for this question: **30 marks**

(a) Describe **two** effects of privation. *(3 marks + 3 marks)*

(b) Describe the findings of **one** study of deprivat/separation and give **one** criticism of this study. *(3 marks + 3 marks)*

(c) To what extent are there cross-cultural variations in attachment? *(18 marks)*

All three parts of each question may be on the same sub-section from the specification or may be drawn from more than one subsection.

Across the two questions for each section/module, all subsections of the content will be sampled.

Each question is divided into three parts.

Part (a) is worth 6 marks and is an **AO1** question.

Part (b) is the same.

Part (c) is worth 18 marks: 6 marks **AO1** and 12 marks **AO2**.

Questions are set with two **assessment objectives** in mind.

Assessment objective 1 (AO1)
Knowledge and understanding of psychology.

Assessment objective 2 (AO2)
Analysis and evaluation of psychology.

Assessment objective 3 (AO3)
To design, conduct and report psychological investigations

This objective is used only for research methods questions.

Questions are only set using the wording of the specification.

Examples

Anything that is given as an *example* (such as Freud) *cannot* be required as part of a question.

Includings

Questions *can* be asked on Loftus' research because this is not given just as a possible example. It is a required topic of study.

Kinds of AO1 questions

Definitions

What is meant by the following terms ... *(2 marks)*
Explain what is meant by ... *(3 marks)*
Describe **two** differences between ... *(3 marks + 3 marks)*

You will only be asked to explain 'definition terms'. These are listed on the next page.

APFCC (aims, procedures, findings, conclusions & criticisms)

Describe the aims and conclusions of **one** study of xxx...*(6 marks)*
Describe the procedures and findings of **one** study of xxx ...*(6 marks)*
Describe the findings of **one** study of xxx and give **one** criticism of this study. *(3 marks + 3 marks)*

Research findings or conclusions

Outline the findings of research into ... *(6 marks)*
Briefly describe the conclusions of research into ... *(6 marks)*

Note that any combination of aims, procedures, findings, conclusions and criticisms is possible.

Note that APFCC questions will only be set on certain topics (see the table on the next page), whereas you could be asked about findings or conclusions in relation to any part of the specification.

Factors, effects & ways

Describe **two** factors that influence ... *(3 marks + 3 marks)*
Describe **two** effects of ... *(3 marks + 3 marks)*
Outline **two** ways that ... *(3 marks + 3 marks)*

Kinds of AO1/AO2 questions

Question possibilities include:

To what extent ...
Consider how psychologists have justified ...
Outline ... and evaluate research into/explanations of ...
Outline ... and consider the strengths and weaknesses ...

In the AO1/AO2 part of the question students are asked to put their psychology into action.

The AO1/AO2 question will sometimes be preceded by a **quotation** – intended to give you some ideas about what you might say.

Examination questions that ask for a definition will only be on the 'key terms' listed below. For each key term you need a '3 mark answer'.

APFCC (aims, procedures, findings, conclusions and criticism) questions will only be set on studies related to certain topics. You must know one study for each of the topics listed.

Cognitive psychology: Memory	Key definitions		APFCC Studies
Capacity	Flashbulb memories	Multi-store model	Duration of STM
Duration	Forgetting	Reconstructive memory	Duration of LTM
Encoding	Long-term memory	Repression	Capacity of STM
Eyewitness testimony	Memory	Short-term memory	Encoding in STM and LTM
			Repressed memories
			Flashbulb memories
			Reconstructive memory
			Eyewitness testimony

Developmental psychology: Attachment	Key definitions		
Attachment	Deprivation	Secure attachment	Secure and insecure attachment
Cognitive development	Insecure attachment	Separation	Cross-cultural variations
Cross-cultural variation	Privation	Social development	Effects of deprivation
Day care			Effects of privation

Physiological psychology: Stress	Key definitions		
Cardiovascular disorders	Life changes	Stress management	Stress and cardiovascular disorders
Control	Physiological approaches to stress management	Stressor	Stress and the immune system
General adaptation syndrome	Psychological approaches to stress management	Workplace stressor	Life changes
Immune system	Stress		Workplace stressors

Individual differences: Abnormality	Key definitions		
Abnormality	Cultural relativism	Eating disorders	Biological explanation of anorexia nervosa
Anorexia nervosa	Deviation from ideal mental health	Failure to function adequately	Psychological explanation of anorexia nervosa
Bulimia nervosa	Deviation from social norms	Statistical infrequency	Biological explanation of bulimia nervosa
			Psychological explanation of bulimia nervosa

Social psychology: Social influence	Key definitions		
Conformity (majority influence)	Ethical issues	Obedience to authority	Conformity (majority influence)
Deception	Experimental validity	Protection of participants from psychological harm	Minority influence
Ecological validity	Informed consent	Resistance to obedience	Obedience to authority
Ethical guidelines	Minority influence	Social influence	

AO1 (assessment objective 1)

AO1 questions are worth 2, 3 or 6 marks. When examiners assess this assessment objective they use one of the mark schemes shown on the right. The 'partial performance' criteria is applied when you are asked to provide more than one of something (such as aims and conclusions of a study), but you only cover one.

For questions worth 2 marks:

2 marks	The answer is both **accurate** and **detailed**.
1 mark	The answer is **basic, lacking detail, muddled** and/or **flawed**.
0 marks	The answer is **inappropriate** or **incorrect**.

For questions worth 3 or 6 marks:

3 marks	6–5 marks	The answer is both **accurate** and **detailed**.
2 marks	4–3 marks	The answer is **limited**. It is generally **accurate** but **less detailed**. (Partial performance is **accurate** and **detailed**).
1 mark	2–1 marks	The answer is **basic, lacking detail, muddled** and/or **flawed**. (Partial performance is **limited, generally accurate** but **less detailed**).
0 marks	0 marks	The answer is **inappropriate** or **incorrect**.

AO2 (assessment objective 2)

This assessment objective is only applied in the part (c) questions. There are three things the examiner looks for when deciding what mark to award: commentary, analysis and effective use of material, as shown in the table.

Commentary. It is sometimes appropriate to offer your own comment upon a piece of research. The more that your comments are informed the more you will receive credit. Simply saying 'It was a good study' lacks information whereas 'This was a good study because it was a well-controlled laboratory experiment' is an informed comment.

Analysis. This means breaking your answer down into its constituent parts. Once you have read the question you need to analyse what you should put in your response. You might identify certain key arguments, studies, examples and so on.

Effective use of material. There is a crucial difference between describing theories, studies and so on and using these to make a point. The descriptive material must be used effectively – you must say what the study contributes to the topic being discussed or what a theory implies.

Marks	Commentary	Analysis	Effective use of material
12–11	There is an **informed** commentary.	**Reasonably thorough analysis** of the relevant psychological studies/methods.	Material has been used in an **effective** manner.
10–9	Reasonable	Slightly limited	Effective
8–7	Reasonable	Limited	Reasonably effective
6–5	Basic	Limited	Reasonably effective
4–3	Superficial	Rudimentary	Minimal interpretation
2–1	Just discernible	Weak and muddled	Mainly irrelevant
0	Absent	Wholly irrelevant	Wholly irrelevant

AO3 (assessment objective 3)

Assessment object 3 (**AO3**) is only used when assessing research methods questions. It is concerned with assessing your ability to *design*, *conduct* and *report* psychological investigation(s) choosing from a range of methods; taking into account the issues of reliability, validity and ethics; and collecting and drawing conclusions from the data.

Most of the research methods questions are assessed using this third objective. Out of 30 marks, 21 marks are assessed in terms of **AO3**. A further 3 marks are **AO1** and the remaining 6 marks are **AO2**. The marking allocation is generally the same as the one used for **AO1**, i.e. accuracy and detail are important.

(in no particular order)

1. **Learn the material** There is no substitute for knowing the facts. However, a clever student finds a way to gain this knowledge efficiently. Use the 'levels of processing approach' – the more you process the information in a meaningful way, the more it will be engraved in your memory without having to sit for hours and try to force the knowledge in.

2. **Process things 'meaningfully'** Do things that mean you have to think about what you are doing, such as writing lists of key words, writing MCQ questions, or delivering a short talk to a group. Organisation, elaboration, effort all lead to deep processing.

3. **In the exam choose your questions carefully** You have a choice in each module of the exam (except research methods) and little time to spare to make this choice. It may make best sense to compare the part (c) questions (as they are worth so many marks).

4. **Manage time effectively in the exam** In the examination you must write no more or less than is indicated by the marks for the question. There is a mark a minute. If a question is worth 6 marks you should spend no more than 6 minutes on your answer. This 6 minutes includes *thinking* as well as writing time.

5. **You should read the question carefully** How many times have you been told this?! But it is true. Candidates see a question with the word '… ethical issues …' and write all they know about ethical issues – but what if the question was about how psychologists *deal* with ethical issues?

6. **Answer only what is required** If you are asked for the procedures and findings of a study, don't include information about the aims and conclusions even if you have spare time. There are no marks for irrelevant material. Use subheadings to focus your attention (e.g. write 'procedures' and 'findings').

7. **The three-point rule** A number of questions ask for one thing (one criticism, one factor, one effect) for 3 marks. Candidates frequently lose marks because they don't provide enough information. For three marks you should (1) name it, (2) provide evidence for your claim in the context of *this* study/theory, and (3) explain why this is a criticism or provide further elaboration. So if your criticism of a study is 'lack of ecological validity' then you have named it. You need to indicate why ecological validity is a problem in this study ('The study tested memory using nonsense words which doesn't reflect how memory is usually used'). Finally you need to further expand your point ('This means that we can't really generalise the findings of this study to real life').

8. **The six-point rule** You may be asked to describe a theory for 6 marks. Revise theories and explanations by identifying six key points which you can elaborate in the exam. This will help your memory too (levels of processing) and provide cues for recall.

9. **The three bears rule** Never write too much or too little. Get it just right: enough detail for all the marks available but not more than this (even if you would like to impress the examiner with all you know). And don't include material that is not relevant.

10. **Manage stress effectively** You have studied stress management (or you should have by the end of the AS year) so apply this knowledge. A moderate level of stress/anxiety is good for performance. An athlete running a race depends on adrenaline to enhance performance. Adrenaline in moderate levels is good for thinking too but too much stress depresses performance. Review your stress management now by writing a list of ways that you might reduce stress in the exam.

11. **Motivate yourself** People do well when they are highly motivated. Find *some* reason for why you really really want to succeed.

Cognitive psychology >	Short- and long-term memory	**Short- and long-term memory**
Developmental psychology >	Forgetting >	Duration
Physiological psychology >		Capacity
Individual differences >	Critical issue:	Encoding
Social psychology >	eyewitness testimony >	Models of memory: Multi-store model
Research methods >		Models of memory: Working memory model
		Models of memory: Levels of processing

KEY DEFINITION

Memory

- The process by which we retain information about events that have happened in the past. This includes:
- Fleeting memories (short-term memories).
- Memories that last for a few hours or days (long-term memories).
- Memories that last a life time (very long-term memories, VLTM).

How are STM and LTM different?

Duration

STM has a very limited duration, probably less than 18 seconds if verbal rehearsal is prevented.

LTM has potentially unlimited duration.

Capacity

STM has a very limited capacity, Miller suggested 7 ± 2 'chunks' of information.

LTM has potentially unlimited capacity.

Encoding

Information in STM is encoded *acoustically* (i.e. represented as *sounds*),

Information in LTM is encoded *semantically* (i.e. represented by its *meaning*).

KEY DEFINITION

Short-term memory

- Your memory for events in the present or immediate past.
- These disappear unless they are rehearsed.
- Limited duration and limited capacity, tends to be acoustically encoded.

KEY DEFINITION

Duration

- A measure of how long a memory lasts before it is no longer available.
- Information in STM lasts only a short time unless it is rehearsed.
- Information in LTM may last forever.

KEY DEFINITION

Capacity

- A measure of the amount that can be held in memory.
- Measured in terms of bits of information such as number of digits or number of chunks.
- STM is a limited capacity store which may explain forgetting (*displacement theory*).

KEY DEFINITION

Encoding

- The way information is changed so it can be stored in memory.
- Information enters the brain via the senses (e.g. eyes and ears) and then is stored in various forms,
- Such as visual codes (like a picture), acoustic forms (sounds), or semantic forms (the meaning of the experience).

KEY DEFINITION

Long-term memory

- Memory for events that have happened in the past, anywhere from 2 minutes to 100 years plus,
- i.e. anything that isn't short-term.
- Potentially unlimited duration and capacity, tends to be semantically encoded.

⟳ PUTTING IT ALL TOGETHER

Memory can be separated into a short-term and a long-term store. These stores differ mainly in terms of duration (a measure of availability), capacity (a measure of bits of information) and encoding (the way information is changed to be stored).

1

Cognitive psychology >
Developmental psychology >
Physiological psychology >
Individual differences >
Social psychology >
Research methods >

Short- and long-term memory
Forgetting >
Critical issue: eyewitness testimony >

Short- and long-term memory
Duration
Capacity
Encoding
Models of memory: Multi-store model
Models of memory: Working memory model
Models of memory: Levels of processing

Duration in STM

starSTUDY on duration in STM   PETERSON & PETERSON (1959)

Aims: To conduct a controlled study to see how long information is retained in STM when verbal rehearsal is prevented.

Procedures: Participants: 24 students. Experimenter said a nonsense trigram followed by a three-digit number for participant to count backwards from until told to stop and recall the nonsense trigram. Repeated 8 times with different retention intervals: 3, 6, 9, 12, 15, or 18 seconds.

Findings: Participants remembered about 90% when there was only a 3 second interval, which dropped to about 20% after 9 seconds and about 2% when there was an 18 second interval.

Conclusions: STM has a duration of less than 18 seconds if verbal rehearsal is prevented. In fact much information has disappeared within a few seconds.

Criticisms: (1) *Ecological validity*: stimulus material artificial and therefore findings may not apply to real life; **(2)** *Population validity*: student participants more intelligent and younger than average.

FACTORS that affect duration in STM

1. **Decay** of the memory trace.
2. **Verbal rehearsal** keeps information in STM.

otherRESEARCH on duration in STM

Study 1   SEBRECHTS ET AL. (1989)

Findings: Participants recalled 3 stimulus words well if tested immediately but recall was almost zero after 4 seconds.

Conclusions: This supports the notion that STM has a very limited duration when data is not rehearsed or processed.

Study 2   REITMAN (1974)

Findings: When participants' attention is diverted, recall of 5 words after 15 secs drops by 24%.

Conclusions: With no rehearsal information still disappears, so limited duration due to spontaneous decay.

FACTORS that affect duration in LTM

1. **Personal significance** of the memory.
2. **Retrieval cues** – memories may be there but can't be brought to mind.

Duration in LTM

starSTUDY on duration in LTM   BAHRICK ET AL. (1975)

Aims: To study personally significant memories to see if VLTM is better than found in laboratory studies.

Procedures: 400 participants aged 17 to 74 asked to list high school classmates' names, recognise classmates' photos, recognise classmates' names.

Findings: 15 years after graduation recognition was 90% accurate for faces and names; after 48 years, it was about 80% for names and 70% for faces. Free recall was poorer: after 15 years was about 60% accurate dropping to 30% after 48 years.

Conclusions: Shows strong evidence for VLTM when memory is for personally significant events. Recognition better than recall, and slightly better for names.

Criticisms: (1) This is a good way to test memory – high *ecological validity*; **(2)** More difficult to control variables e.g. whether they saw classmates regularly.

otherRESEARCH on duration in LTM

Study 1
SHEPARD (1967)

Findings: Participants could recognise almost all of 600 specially chosen 'memorable' pictures when viewed again after one hour, and 50% after 4 months.

Conclusions: Shows that recognition memory very good over the long term, at least for memorable material.

Study 2
WAGANAAR AND GRONENEWEG (1990)

Findings: Concentration camp survivors had good recall for many but not all details after 30 years.

Conclusions: Shows that some memories are enduring, possibly just those that are personally significant.

Cognitive psychology >	Short and long-term memory >	Short- and long-term memory
Developmental psychology >	Forgetting >	Duration
Physiological psychology >		**Capacity**
Individual differences >	Critical issue:	Encoding
Social psychology >	eyewitness testimony >	Models of memory: Multi-store model
Research methods >		Models of memory: Working memory model
		Models of memory: Levels of processing

Capacity in STM

starSTUDY on capacity in STM   JACOBS (1887)

Aims: To demonstrate how much information could be stored in STM using the serial digit span.

Procedures: The *serial digit span technique* was used (repeating back a string of increasing items in the correct order). Participants were given letters and numbers omitting those with two syllables (W and 7).

Findings: The average span for digits was 9.3 items whereas it was 7.3 for letters. Digit span increased steadily with age: 8 year olds remembered 6.6 digits and 19 year olds remembered 8.6 digits.

Conclusions: Shows that STM does have a limited capacity of somewhere between 5 and 9 items depending on the material used (letters or digits) and age. Digits might be easier to recall because there were 9 digits whereas there were 25 letters.

Criticisms: (1) Supported by subsequent research; **(2)** The individual differences in recall suggests that one is not just measuring capacity but other strategies that influence capacity such as chunking.

FACTORS that affect capacity in STM

1. **Chunking** increases capacity.
2. **Size of chunk** – larger chunks lead to lower capacity

otherRESEARCH on capacity in STM

Study 1   MILLER (1956)

Findings: Found, from reviewing other studies, that people remember 5 letters as well as they can recall 5 words.

Conclusions: Chunking is vital to reduce the load on STM and remember more things at one time.

Study 2   SIMON (1974)

Findings: People have shorter span for longer chunks (such as 8 word phrases) than smaller chunks.

Conclusions: Chunking isn't as straightforward as suggested by Miller, the size of the chunk does affect STM.

Capacity in LTM

RESEARCH on capacity in LTM

Study 1   MERKLE (1988)

Findings: A calculation of capacity based on the number of synapses in the brain, memory may be in the range $10^{13} - 10^{15}$ links, or between one thousand and one million gigabytes.

Conclusions: Relatively small compared to most computers but human brain more organised.

Study 2
TULVING (1962)

Findings: In a study of forgetting they found that each time participants recalled a word list, the words differed though the response rate was the same (about 50%).

Conclusions: This suggests that memories are there but not always accessible. Such variability makes it impossible to test the capacity of LTM because memories may be there but not accessible.

FACTORS that affect capacity in LTM

1. **'More synapses'** means greater capacity.
2. **Lack of retrieval cues** – disguise real capacity.

Cognitive psychology >	Short- and long-term memory	Short- and long-term memory
Developmental psychology >	Forgetting >	Duration
Physiological psychology >	Critical issue:	Capacity
Individual differences >	eyewitness testimony >	**Encoding**
Social psychology >		Models of memory: Multi-store model
Research methods >		Models of memory: Working memory model
		Models of memory: Levels of processing

starSTUDY on encoding in STM and LTM   BADDELEY (1966)

Aims: To confirm Conrad's (1964) finding that STM was affected by acoustic confusions and investigate whether the same applied to LTM, and to see if either memory store was affected by semantic confusions.

Testing STM

Procedures: Four groups, each group heard one word list (acoustically similar or dissimilar, semantically similar or dissimilar). This list was repeated four times, each time participants were shown a list of the words jumbled up and asked to recall them in the correct order.

Findings: Participants with acoustic similarity did worst. On trial 4 they recalled about 55% of the words. Whereas participants with the other three lists recalled about 75% of the words.

Conclusions: Words in STM remembered in terms of their sounds (acoustically).

Testing LTM

Procedures: Same except this time recall was after a 20 minute retention interval during which the participants performed another task.

Findings: Participants with semantic similarity did worst. On trial 4 they recalled about 55% of the words. Whereas participants with the other three lists recalled at least 70% of the words.

Conclusions: Words in LTM tend to be coded in terms of their meaning (semantically).

Criticisms: (1) Some experiments show visual codes also used in STM, e.g. Brandimote *et al.* (below); **(2)** Relevant to memory for words (*semantic memory*), not other kinds of memory e.g. *episodic memory* (memory for events).

FACTORS that affect encoding in STM

1. **Acoustic similarity** – reduces recall.

2. **Nature of stimulus** – some items lend themselves less well to acoustic coding

FACTORS that affect encoding in LTM

1. **Semantic similarity** – reduces recall.

2. **Age** – older people use more active encoding strategies that younger people.

otherRESEARCH on encoding in memory

Study 1   BRANDIMOTE ET AL. (1992)

Findings: Participants used visual encoding in STM if they were given a visual task (pictures) and prevented from doing any verbal rehearsal in the retention interval.

Conclusions: Shows that STM not exclusively acoustic; it's related to task and intervening activities.

Study 2   POSNER (1969)

Findings: Participants were slower when they had to say whether two letters were the same if the letters were Aa rather than AA.

Conclusions: This suggests that they must have been processing the data visually rather than acoustically because 'A' and 'a' sound the same and should take equally long.

PUTTING IT ALL TOGETHER

Research supports the distinction between STM and LTM in terms of duration (less than 18 seconds or forever), capacity (7 ± 2 or infinite), and encoding (acoustic or semantic).

Cognitive psychology	>	Short and long-term memory>	Short- and long-term memory
Developmental psychology	>	Forgetting	>	Duration
Physiological psychology	>			Capacity
Individual differences	>	Critical issue:		Encoding
Social psychology	>	eyewitness testimony	>	**Models of memory: Multi-store model**
Research methods	>			Models of memory: Working memory model
				Models of memory: Levels of processing

EXPLANATION of the multi-store model (MSM)

ATKINSON AND SHIFFRIN (1968)

- An explanation of how memory processes work based on the idea that there are three separate stores (SM, STM, LTM).

- SM (sensory memory) is equivalent to any one of the senses e.g. the eye or ear. STM and LTM are defined on page 1.

- Each store has unique characteristics in terms of duration, capacity and encoding.

- Information first arrives at the senses. If attention is focused on it, it is transferred to STM.

- Information is maintained in STM through rehearsal otherwise it will decay. It also may be displaced by new information.

- Increasing rehearsal leads to transfer from STM to LTM, the more rehearsal the better it is remembered.

KEY DEFINITION

Multi-store model

- An explanation of memory based on memory stores.

- Information transferred from SM to STM due to attention.

- Information transferred from STM to LTM due to rehearsal.

RESEARCH related to the MSM

EVALUATION

Strengths

1. Research support e.g. studies of duration, capacity and encoding.

2. Matches commonsense perception of memory.

Limitations

1. An oversimplification e.g. doesn't distinguish between different STM stores (see *working memory*) and different LTM stores (*episodic* and *procedural memory*).

2. Rehearsal doesn't explain all LTM memories (e.g. flashbulb memories).

Study 1
SPERLING (1960)

Findings: When asked (after 50 milliseconds) to report 12 letters/digits from a display recall was poorer (5 items recalled, about 42%) than when asked to give one row only (3 items recalled, 75%).

Conclusions: This shows that information decays rapidly in the sensory store.

Study 2
GLANZER AND CUNITZ (1966)

Findings: Participants best remember words from start of list (*primacy effect*) and end of list (*recency*).

Conclusions: Called the *serial position effect* which occurs because first words best rehearsed and transferred to LTM, last words are in STM when you start recalling the list.

Study 3
BEARDSLEY (1997) AND SQUIRE ET AL. (1992)

Findings: Using brain scanning techniques found that STM associated with activity in prefrontal cortex active, LTM associated with hippocampus.

Conclusions: Shows that stores are distinct.

PUTTING IT ALL TOGETHER

Research shows that memory does consist of a series of different stores (SM, STM and LTM) linked by rehearsal, as described by the multi-store model. However there is more to memory than this; the multi-store model is only part of the story.

According to this model,
FACTORS that affect memory :

1. **Attention**

2. **Rehearsal**

Cognitive psychology >	Short and long-term memory >	Short- and long-term memory
Developmental psychology >	Forgetting >	Duration
Physiological psychology >		Capacity
Individual differences >	Critical issue:	Encoding
Social psychology >	eyewitness testimony >	Models of memory: Multi-store model
Research methods >		**Models of memory: Working memory model**
		Models of memory: Levels of processing

EXPLANATION of the working memory model (WM)

BADDELEY AND HITCH (1974)

- An explanation of immediate memory (STM) i.e. the memory used when working on something.

- *Central executive* acts like attention, has limited capacity.

- *Phonological loop* deals with auditory information and preserves the order of information.

- Subdivided into *phonological store* (inner ear) and *articulatory process* (inner voice).

- *Visuo-spatial sketchpad* stores visual and/or spatial information when engaged in such tasks.

- Explains how simultaneous performance of two visual tasks interfere with each other, but not when one task is visual and the other auditory.

According to this model,

FACTORS that affect memory

1. **Kind of task** performed (verbal or visual)

2. **Duration of task** – phonological loop limited

EVALUATION

Strengths

1. Explains why it is easier to do two tasks that are different (verbal and visual) than doing two tasks that are similar.

2. Explains the *word length effect* (people remember more short words than long words when STM tested).

Limitations

1. Central executive is not clearly defined and doesn't really explain any particular activity.

2. May be more than one component in the central executive.

RESEARCH related to WM model

Study 1
HITCH AND BADDELEY (1976)

Findings: Task occupying the central executive was performed more slowly when participants had to perform a second task involving both the central executive and the articulatory loop, than articulatory loop alone. Performance was affected equally by a task just using the articulatory loop or no extra task.

Conclusions: Doing two tasks involving the same component causes difficulty. When different components are used performance not affected.

Study 2
BADDELEY ET AL. (1975)

Findings: Phonological loop holds the amount of information that you can say in 2 seconds. But the *word length effect* (see right) disappears if a person is given an articulatory suppression task (a repetitive task that ties up the articulatory process).

Conclusions: *Word length effect* is evidence of the phonological loop (finite space for rehearsal related to what can be said) and articulatory suppression task is evidence of the articulatory process.

Study 3
BADDELEY ET AL. (1975)

Findings: Participants had more difficulty doing two visual tasks simultaneously (track light and describe letter F) than a visual and verbal task.

Conclusion: Evidence of visuo-spatial sketchpad.

PUTTING IT ALL TOGETHER

The working memory model is a refinement of the multi-store model, describing what is happening in immediate storage in terms of a further set of stores specialised for auditory and visual information.

Cognitive psychology >	Short and long-term memory >	Short- and long-term memory
Developmental psychology >	Forgetting >	Duration
Physiological psychology >		Capacity
Individual differences >	Critical issue:	Encoding
Social psychology >	eyewitness testimony >	Models of memory: Multi-store model
Research methods >		Models of memory: Working memory model
		Models of memory: Levels of processing

EXPLANATION of levels of processing approach (LOP)

CRAIK AND LOCKHART (1972)

- An explanation of memory focusing on how information is processed rather than suggesting there are different stores.

- Things that are processed more deeply (meaningfully) become more memorable.

- 'Depth' can be achieved through increasingly complex interaction with information-to-be-remembered (e.g. semantic processing, organisation, distinctiveness, elaboration, and effort).

- Memory is an automatic by-product of processing.

- Primary memory is like STM except it is a flexible processing activity rather than a limited store.

- Enduring memories (LTM) are created through deep encoding processes.

According to this model,
FACTORS that affect memory

1. **Depth**
2. **Meaning**

RESEARCH related to LOP approach

Information can be processed more deeply through semantic processing, organisation, distinctiveness, elaboration and effort.

Study 1
CRAIK AND TULVING (1975)

Semantic processing
Findings: Words remembered best if processed by meaning (deep processing) and least if processed by physical structure (shallow). Analysis of sound (phonemic) was intermediate.

Study 2
MANDLER (1967)

Organisation
Findings: Participants could recall words after being asked to sort words repeatedly into piles. Best recall was by those who had used most categories.

Study 3
EYSENCK AND EYSENCK (1980)

Distinctiveness
Findings: Words said in distinctive way (e.g. c-o-m-b) more memorable.

Study 4
PALMERE ET AL. (1983)

Elaboration
Findings: Recall of information was higher for the ideas expressed in the elaborated paragraphs.

Study 5
TYLER ET AL. (1979)

Effort
Findings: Participants recalled more difficult anagrams better in an unexpected test.

EVALUATION

Strengths

1. Supported by research studies (see left).

2. Explains why we remember things without rehearsal, such as *episodic* memories.

Limitations

1. Recall depends on what you are required to recall. In a rhyming recognition test recall better for words phonemically processed (Morris et al., 1977). Called *transfer-appropriate processing*. Lockhart and Craik (1990) say that depth refers to greater processing within the relevant domain.

2. The definition is circular. Something is remembered if it is deeply processed; deep processing leads to better memory. However, the concept of 'depth' has been refined.

⟲ PUTTING IT ALL TOGETHER

The levels of processing approach emphasises processes rather than storage compartments, suggesting that the more information is processed the more it is remembered.

Cognitive psychology >
Developmental psychology >
Physiological psychology >
Individual differences >
Social psychology >
Research methods >

Short and long-term memory>
Forgetting >
Critical issue:
eyewitness testimony >

Forgetting in STM
Forgetting in LTM
Emotional factors: Flashbulb memory
Emotional factors: Repression

KEY DEFINITION

Forgetting

- The inability to recall or recognise something that has previously been learned.

- May be lack of availability, e.g. decay when the *memory trace* has disappeared.

- May be lack of accessibility, e.g. cue-dependent forgetting when the memory is stored somewhere but can't be found at that time.

FACTORS that explain forgetting in STM

1. **Decay** – information lost

2. **Displacement** – information lost

EXPLANATION 1
Decay theory

Explanation

Trace disappears if not rehearsed. This would explain results from Peterson and Peterson (page 2). No rehearsal, no memory in STM after 18 seconds.

Research support   REITMAN (1974)

Findings: When participants' attention diverted to prevent rehearsal (listening for a tone), recall dropped by 24%.

Conclusions: There is evidence for decay – except that we can't be entirely certain that new information had not entered STM.

EXPLANATION 2
Displacement theory

Explanation

Existing information displaced (pushed out or overwritten) by newer information because STM is a limited-capacity store.

Research support   WAUGH AND NORMAN (1965)

Findings: If the probe (in a *serial probe task*) was early in the list, recall was poor (less than 20%). If the probe came near the end of the list, recall was good (over 80%).

Conclusions: Supports displacement theory because forgetting must be due to the fact that subsequent numbers increasingly displaced.

EVALUATION

Difficult to prevent rehearsal (to demonstrate decay) without introducing information that will overwrite (displace) original information (In Peterson and Peterson experiment counting digits in retention interval might have displaced the original nonsense trigrams).

EVALUATION

In *serial probe task*, if numbers read faster (4 per sec.) rather than slower (1 per sec.), recall was better. Must be due to decay because displacement would not have been affected by timing (Waugh and Norman, 1965).

Decay *and* displacement

Shallice (1967) (using the *serial probe technique*) also found that forgetting was less if the numbers were presented faster, but found a stronger effect for moving the position of the probe. This suggests that displacement and decay explain forgetting in STM but that displacement is more important.

⟳ PUTTING IT ALL TOGETHER

It appears that forgetting in STM is more likely to be due to decay rather than displacement – though this presumes that information has been placed in STM in the first place.

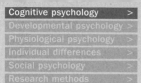

Cognitive psychology >	Short and long-term memory>	Forgetting in STM
Developmental psychology >	Forgetting >	**Forgetting in LTM**
Physiological psychology >	Critical issue:	Emotional factors: Flashbulb
Individual differences >	eyewitness testimony >	memory
Social psychology >		Emotional factors: Repression
Research methods >		

EXPLANATION 1
Decay theory

Explanation
Physical memory is lost through brain damage or as brain atrophies or through ageing process.

Research support
Lashley (1931) found a correlation between the amount of material removed from rats' brains and the amount they forgot.

EVALUATION

1. Decay can't explain why some memories are very long-lasting (e.g. flashbulb memories).

2. Baddeley and Hitch (1977) studied rugby players; the more games they had played over a season the more they forgot (proportionately). Supports interference theory. If decay theory was correct all players should recall similar percentage of games.

EXPLANATION 2
Interference theory

Explanation
One memory gets in the way of another memory, preventing retrieval.

Proactive interference (PI) past learning interferes with current learning.

Retroactive interference (RI) current learning interferes with past learning.

Research support
Underwood (1957) found evidence for both using *paired associate technique*.

EVALUATION

1. Interference requires special conditions (e.g. similar stimulus paired with two different responses) not common in everyday life.

2. Tulving and Pstotka (1971) found the more lists a participant learned, the worse their performance (retroactive interference) but if they were given cues (category names) then recall was a fairly constant 70% for all lists no matter how many were learned. Evidence for cue-dependent forgetting.

EXPLANATION 3
Cue-dependent forgetting

Explanation
Forgetting due to retrieval failure because a person fails to successfully recover something from memory that was previously learned. Specific cues may help retrieve it.

The *encoding specificity principle* states that the closer the cue to the original thing, the more useful it will be.

Research support
External cues: context-dependent learning e.g. Abernethy (1940) found recall better when tested in classroom where learning took place.

Internal cues: state-dependent learning e.g. Goodwin et al. (1969) found recall better when in drunken state again. Aggleton and Waskett (1999) found smell was an effective retrieval cue when testing recall at Jorvik Viking Centre.

EVALUATION

1. Powerful explanation for forgetting. Some psychologists (e.g. Eysenck, 1998) believe this is the main reason for forgetting in LTM.

2. Many of the studies are laboratory-based and not very like everyday memory, e.g. cues don't explain forgetting in *procedural memory*.

FACTORS that explain forgetting in LTM

1. **Decay** – information lost

2. **Interference** – information gets in the way

3. **Retrieval failure** (cue-dependent forgetting)

⟳ PUTTING IT ALL TOGETHER

There are many reasons for forgetting in LTM, each related to particular circumstances: decay explains the effects of ageing and brain damage, interference explains special situations involving similar conditions, and cue-dependent forgetting explains how we sometimes can't bring a memory to mind though we know it is there (a problem of accessibility rather than availability).

Cognitive psychology >
Developmental psychology >
Physiological psychology >
Individual differences >
Social psychology >
Research methods >

Short and long-term memory >
Forgetting >
Critical issue:
eyewitness testimony >

Forgetting in STM
Forgetting in LTM
Emotional factors: Flashbulb memory
Emotional factors: Repression

EXPLANATIONS of flashbulb memory

1. **Emotion:** personal significance, consequentiality, surprise all create arousal which produce hormones which affect memory (Cahill and McGaugh, 1998).

2. **Rehearsal:** such memories become deeply ingrained because they are constantly revisited and rehearsed (Neisser, 1982).

[These are also **factors** that affect flashbulb memory.]

starSTUDY on flashbulb memory   BROWN AND KULIK (1977)

Aims: To investigate what kind of events generate flashbulb memories (FBs). Might this be related to race (e.g. black participants remember black events better = personal significance)?

Procedures: Volunteer sample of 40 white, 40 black Americans given questionnaire listing 10 national events and asked to recall circumstances when they heard about it.

Findings: White people had greater recall for events concerning white individuals, same true for black individuals. Almost everyone had FBs surrounding JFK's death, about 50% (black and white) had FBs for RFK's death; 75% black people and 33% white people had FBs for Martin Luther King.

Conclusions: The race effect supports the view that personal 'consequentiality' is important. 'Surprise' also seems to be an important factor, which is also related to emotion.

Criticisms: (1) But emotion sometimes leads to poorer recall e.g. repressed memory; **(2)** Some studies find FBs no different to other memories (see below).

KEY DEFINITION

Flashbulb memory

- A special kind of memory where an individual has a detailed and enduring recollection.

- Such recollections relate to personally significant events.

- What is recalled is the *context* in which the person first heard about the event, not the event itself.

otherRESEARCH for flashbulb memory

Study 1
SHEINGOLD AND TENNEY (1982)

Findings: Most people had FBs for personal memories, such as the birth of a brother or sister.

Study 2
JOHNSON AND SCOTT (1978)

Findings: Participants in high stress condition (man with bloody letter-opener) had better recall.

RESEARCH *against* flashbulb memory

Study 1
SCHMOLCK ET AL. (2000)

Findings: Students' FBs for OJ Simpson trial were 50% accurate after 15 months, and 29% accurate after 32 months, and contained 11% and 40% distortions respectively.

Conclusions: FBs do decay and are not enduringly accurate (may not have been FBs).

Study 2
WRIGHT (1993)

Findings: After 5 months people had rather vague memories about Hillsborough disaster.

Conclusions: Most people reconstructed memories, blending real experiences with accounts they read.

PUTTING IT ALL TOGETHER

People do recall the context of hearing about a personally significant event but it is difficult to know whether such memories are really any different from memory generally (i.e. more accurate or enduring).

Cognitive psychology >	Short and long-term memory >	Forgetting in STM
Developmental psychology >	Forgetting >	Forgetting in LTM
Physiological psychology >	Critical issue: eyewitness testimony >	Emotional factors: Flashbulb memory
Individual differences >		Emotional factors: Repression
Social psychology >		
Research methods >		

KEY DEFINITION

Repression

- A way of dealing with memories for traumatic events so that the associated anxiety is not experienced.

- The memory for the event is placed beyond conscious awareness.

- This displacement makes one feel better, but may affect thought and action.

EXPLANATIONS of repression

1. **Freud** suggested that repression is an unconscious *ego-defence mechanism* to prevent the ego being threatened by anxiety aroused by certain memories.

2. **Suppression**: a more intentional coping strategy for dealing with the unpleasant memories of a traumatic event.

starSTUDY on repression

WILLIAMS (1994)

Aims: To investigate recovered memories. Are they 'real' (repressed and are now recovered) or did the events never happen (i.e. are false memories)?

Procedures: Over 100 women interviewed who had attended city hospital emergency room 20 years previously for sexual assault. Both participants and interviewers told this was a follow-up study of the health of women who had received medical care from the city hospital during childhood (i.e. double blind). No direct questions were asked about sexual abuse.

Findings: 38% showed no recall for earlier sexual abuse. Of those who did recall the abuse, 16% said they had repressed it at some time. Abuse at an earlier age was more likely to be forgotten.

Conclusions: Repressed memories are common. Recovery of memories is possible. Age may reduce ability to remember.

Criticisms: **(1)** Biased sample: poor urban women; **(2)** Possible that some of initial reports had been fictitious or that women didn't want to talk about abuse (however those rated as most credible had highest level of forgetting, which supports repression).

otherRESEARCH for repression

Study 1
BRADLEY AND BADDELEY (1990)

Findings: Participants had more difficulty recalling words associated with emotionally charged trigger words but, after a month, remembered emotionally associated pairs better than other associations.

Conclusions: Possible that anxiety depresses STM but enhances LTM. Or repression disappears over time.

Study 2
MYERS AND BREWIN (1994)

Findings: Repressors took twice as long to recall their unhappy memories; age of first negative memory was older than for non-repressors.

Conclusions: Repressors have more anxiety-provoking memories; may be 'suppression' rather than true repression.

Study 3
KARON AND WIDENER (1997)

Findings: WWII veterans recovered from mental illness when traumas remembered in therapy.

RESEARCH *against* repression

Study 1
HOCHMAN (1994)

Findings: A study of children whose school was attacked by a sniper showed that even some who were not present at the time of the attack still had vivid ('false') memories of the event.

Conclusions: Shows that traumatic events (Post Traumatic Stress Disorder (PTSD)) 'haunt' victims and are not repressed.

Study 2
HOLMES (1990)

Conclusions: Review of 60 years of repression research concluded no evidence that unequivocally supports repression.

↻ **PUTTING IT ALL TOGETHER**

Some traumatic experiences are not repressed (they are recalled more frequently) and some traumatic experiences are more accurately described as 'suppressed' – though suppression may serve the same psychological function as repression.

11

Cognitive psychology >	Short and long-term memory >	**Eyewitness testimony, including Loftus' research**
Developmental psychology >	Forgetting >	
Physiological psychology >	Critical issue: eyewitness testimony >	Reconstructive memory
Individual differences >		
Social psychology >		
Research methods >		

starSTUDY on eyewitness testimony

LOFTUS AND PALMER (1974)

Aims: Investigate the accuracy of memory after witnessing a car accident, to see if leading questions distort the accuracy of eyewitnesses' immediate recall.

Procedures: Forty-five students shown films of traffic accidents. Questions afterwards included a critical one about speed of car containing word hit, smashed, collided, bumped or contacted.

Findings: The group with 'smashed' estimated the highest speed (about 41 m.p.h.), the group given the word 'contacted' estimated the lowest speed (about 30 m.p.h.).

Conclusions: Leading questions (post-event information) can have a significant effect on memory (could be on original memory or recall).

Criticisms: (1) Not true to life, recall more accurate in real life (Yuille and Cutshall, 1986); **(2)** *Demand characteristics* – very hard to estimate speed so use any available clue.

KEY DEFINITION

Eyewitness testimony (EWT)

- The evidence provided in court by a person who witnessed a crime.

- Usually used to identify the perpetrator of the crime.

- The accuracy of eyewitness recall may be affected during initial encoding, subsequent storage and/or eventual retrieval.

otherRESEARCH from Loftus

Study 1
LOFTUS AND PALMER (1974)

Findings: Tested a different set of participants after a week and those given 'smashed' were more likely to recollect broken glass (there was none).

Conclusions: Shows effect of post-event information on later recall.

Study 2
LOFTUS (1979)

Findings: Participants heard a discussion and then one man appeared. Later identification 49% accurate when man holding pen, 33% accurate when man holding bloody paper knife.

Conclusions: Demonstrates *weapon focus* which might explain why recall sometimes is poor.

otherRESEARCH on eyewitness testimony

Study 1
BEKERIAN AND BOWERS (1983)

Findings: Participants given a question that matched the slide they were shown (stop or yield sign) gave more accurate recall when questions were consistent than inconsistent. But when the slides were presented in the right sequence, misleading information (inconsistent question) had no effect.

Conclusions: Misleading questions (post-event information) affect *retrieval* rather than storage.

Study 2
LINDSAY (1990)

Findings: When told to ignore misleading information in an account of a crime, participants still affected by misleading information.

Conclusions: In this study leading questions changed *storage*!

FACTORS that affect EWT

1. **Memory for certain personal characteristics** is accurate (e.g. gender, race, hair colour) but not for age and height.

2. **Arousal:** moderate levels lead to good recall; low and high levels interfere with accuracy.

3. **ADVOKATE:** Amount of time, Distance, Visibility, Obstructions, Know, Any reason to remember, Time, Errors.

⟳ PUTTING IT ALL TOGETHER

Leading questions may alter recall (initial storage or retrieval) but probably only for certain kinds of information (e.g. speed of a car or height of a criminal). Other factors matter too, such as weapon focus (reduces recall) and arousal.

Cognitive psychology >	Short and long-term memory >	Eyewitness testimony, including Loftus' research
Developmental psychology >	Forgetting >	
Physiological psychology >	Critical issue: eyewitness testimony >	Reconstructive memory
Individual differences >		
Social psychology >		
Research methods >		

EXPLANATION of reconstructive memory

- Memory is not simply reproduction.
- We store **fragments** of information.
- At recall these fragments are reconstructed into a meaningful whole.
- Past experience and beliefs shape this reconstruction.
- **Schema** store information about past experience and beliefs.
- Schema may affect encoding as well as recall.

starSTUDY on reconstructive memory

BARTLETT (1932)

Aims: To see how cultural expectations affect memory and lead to predictable distortions.

Procedures: Repeated reproductions: showing a story (e.g. War of the ghosts) or simple drawing to a participant and asking them to recall it repeatedly over days and months. Stimulus material should belong to a different culture.

Findings: Stories were shortened, phrases changed to match own culture, recalled version became fixed but always slight variations.

Conclusions: We remember fragments and use our knowledge of social situations to reconstruct memory, an efficient system. Memory is a social act.

Criticisms: (1) Not well controlled, if accuracy was stressed then errors much reduced (Gauld and Stephenson, 1967); **(2)** Recall of real life events more accurate (Wynn and Logie, 1998).

otherRESEARCH on reconstructive memory

Study 1
CARMICHAEL ET AL. (1932)

Findings: Recall of objects was related to labels given to each set of participants e.g. crescent or 'C'.

Conclusions: The label creates expectations (schema) which affect memory.

Study 2
BRANSFORD AND JOHNSON (1972)

Findings: Participants who were given the title ('Making and flying a kite') did better at recall of text.

Conclusions: Having a schema (title) helps encode information.

KEY DEFINITION

Reconstructive memory

- Fragments of stored information are reassembled during recall.
- The gaps are filled in by our expectations and beliefs (schema) which are often socially constructed.
- The end product is a coherent narrative.

EVALUATION

Strengths

1. Explains effect of stereotypes and schema on recall.
2. Good research support.

Limitations

1. Memory can be very accurate.
2. Highly incongruous items may be more memorable (Brewer and Treyens, 1981).

FACTORS that affect reconstructive memory

1. **Stereotypes** – create expectations.
2. **Interviewing techniques** bias what is recalled.

PUTTING IT ALL TOGETHER

Schema assist initial storage or retrieval by organising information, but this organisation inevitably changes what we remember along the lines of our stereotypes/schema. Not all memories are stored in this way.

Cognitive psychology	>	The development and		The development of attachments
Developmental psychology	>	variety of attachments	>	Individual differences: secure/insecure
Physiological psychology	>	Deprivation and privation	>	Individual differences: cross-cultural
Individual differences	>	Critical issue: Day care	>	variations
Social psychology	>			Explanations of attachment
Research methods	>			

KEY DEFINITION

Attachment

- An emotional bond between two people, especially mother and infant.

- Maintains physical closeness between mother and infant.

- Promotes healthy emotional development.

The DEVELOPMENT of attachments (a stage theory)

1. **Pre-attachment** (0–2 months). Little discrimination between familiar and unfamiliar people.

2. **Attachment-in-the-making** (2–7 months). Recognition of familiar people but no stranger anxiety.

3. **Specific** *attachments* (approx. 7 months). *Separation protest* and *stranger anxiety* develop.

4. **Multiple attachments** (soon after). One main attachment figure (*monotropy*) but others too.

5. **Reciprocal relationships**. Predicting and controlling responses of caregiver.

RESEARCH on the development of attachments

Study 1
SCHAFFER AND EMERSON (1964)

Findings: Most infants showed *separation protest* and *stranger anxiety* at around the age of 7 months, sign of specific attachment. Within 1 month multiple attachments followed. For 39% of infants the primary caregiver was not the one who spent most time with infant. Responsiveness of caregiver was related to strength of attachment.

Conclusions: Supports the stage theory above and *caregiver sensitivity hypothesis*; doesn't support *cupboard love theory*.

Study 2
AINSWORTH (1963 AND 1964)

Findings: Observations of infants in Uganda and Baltimore, USA: infants seek to be close to their mothers especially at times when they are threatened by something in the environment.

Conclusions: Such behaviour is adaptive: proximity-seeking keeps infant safe and using parent as safe base is important for exploratory behaviour and cognitive development.

FACTORS that influence the development of attachments

1. **Good mothering**
   Sensitive mothers have secure children (*caregiver sensitivity hypothesis*).

2. **Child's contribution**
   Infants with easy temperaments are easier to get on with (the *temperament hypothesis*).

PUTTING IT ALL TOGETHER

The development of attachment follows a predictable – and probably universal – sequence which is not surprising as it is an adaptive behaviour and therefore likely to be genetic. Quality rather than quantity of parenting creates stronger and more secure attachment.

Cognitive psychology >	The development and variety of attachments >	The development of attachments
Developmental psychology >		Individual differences: secure/insecure
Physiological psychology >	Deprivation and privation >	Individual differences: cross-cultural variations
Individual differences >	Critical issue: Day care >	
Social psychology >		Explanations of attachment
Research methods >		

EFFECTS of secure and insecure attachment

1. **Behaviour at school** e.g. problem solving, self-confidence, popularity.
2. **Adult romantic behaviour** See Hazan and Shaver, below.

EXPLANATIONS of secure and insecure attachment

1. **Internal working model** Relationship with caregiver acts as template for later relationships.
2. **Temperament hypothesis** Innate personality characteristics determine attachment type, not caregiver sensitivity.

STARstudy on secure and insecure attachment
AINSWORTH ET AL. (1978)

Aims: To test infant behaviour in a situation of mild stress and novelty.

Procedures: Strange Situation consists of 8 episodes with stranger, mother and infant in a laboratory. Observations recorded of willingness to explore, stranger anxiety, separation anxiety, behaviour at reunion and caregiver's behaviour.

Findings: 66% securely attached, 22% avoidant, 12% resistant. Securely attached and insecurely attached infants behaved as described on right.

Conclusions: There are individual differences which are related to mothers' behaviour.

Criticisms: (1) Widely used method of assessing attachment. (2) Ethical concerns about stress to infants. (3) Classification may lack validity (applies to relationship not child; applies to US culture only).

otherRESEARCH on secure and insecure attachment

Study 1 **HAZAN AND SHAVER (1987)**

Findings: Answers to the 'love quiz': insecure/avoidant adults found it difficult to trust others, felt nervous about getting too close. Insecure/resistant adults worried that partners didn't love them and wanted to merge with another. Secure adults experienced close relationships, felt comfortable being depended upon and didn't worry about being abandoned.

Conclusions: Early attachment experiences are related to adult romantic behaviours. Also related to attitudes towards love. This may be caused by the *internal working model* developed through relationship with main caregiver.

Study 2 **BELSKY AND ROVINE (1987)**

Findings: Infants who showed signs of behavioural instability (e.g. shaking) were less likely to become securely attached to their mothers.

Conclusions: Supports the *temperament hypothesis*.

PUTTING IT ALL TOGETHER

Infants differ in terms of their attachment styles, which can be assessed in the Strange Situation. This classification can be used to investigate what causes secure attachment (e.g. sensitive caregiving or temperament) and the effects of secure attachment (e.g. certain adult romantic styles).

Cognitive psychology >	The development and variety of attachments >	The development of attachments
Developmental psychology >		Individual differences: secure/insecure
Physiological psychology >	Deprivation and privation >	**Individual differences: cross-cultural variations**
Individual differences >	Critical issue: Day care >	
Social psychology >		Explanations of attachment
Research methods >		

starSTUDY on cross-cultural variations in attachment

VAN IJZENDOORN & KROONENBERG (1988)

Aims: To see if there are different patterns of attachment in different countries and within the same country.

Procedures: Meta-analysis of 32 studies that used the Strange Situation; 8 different countries.

Findings: Variation between countries was small. Secure classification was most common. Variation within countries was 1.5 times larger than between cultures.

Conclusions: The US pattern of attachment is the norm, suggesting that this is the best for healthy emotional development.

Criticisms: (1) The *Strange Situation* is not valid in all cultures; **(2)** Countries are not the same as cultures.

KEY DEFINITION

Cross-cultural variations

- The way that behaviour differs from one culture to another.

- A culture is a group of people with shared social practices, such as child-rearing.

- These practices affect development and behaviour leading to cultural variations.

otherRESEARCH on cross-cultural variations in attachment

Study 1
GROSSMANN AND GROSSMANN (1991)

Findings: More German infants classified as insecure.

Conclusions: Could be due to different child-rearing practices in Germany, that value interpersonal difference.

Study 2
TRONICK ET AL. (1992)

Findings: Children most attached to mothers despite multiple caregiving.

Conclusions: Supports concept of *monotropy* across cultures.

Study 3
FOX (1977)

Findings: Children raised by metapelets (on Kibbutzim) still most securely attached to mother.

Conclusions: Quality not quantity of care is what matters for attachment.

FACTORS that affect cross-cultural variations in attachment

1. **The role of the mother** Care by mothers at home is (or was) the norm in some cultures, may explain differences.

2. **Individualist and collectivist** Individualist cultures expect children to become independent; collectivist cultures encourage dependence which would affect behaviour in the *Strange Situation*.

⟳ PUTTING IT ALL TOGETHER

There are cultural differences in infant attachment styles, which can be related to local child-rearing practices. There are also similarities, which may be explained with reference to the adaptive and inherited nature of attachment. However, the research may be meaningless because the Strange Situation is not valid in all cultures.

Cognitive psychology >	The development and variety of attachments >	The development of attachments
Developmental psychology >		Individual differences: secure/insecure
Physiological psychology >	Deprivation and privation >	Individual differences: cross-cultural variations
Individual differences >	Critical issue: Day care >	
Social psychology >		Explanations of attachment
Research methods >		

EXPLANATION 1 The behaviourist approach: Learning theory (cupboard love theory)

Classical conditioning. Learning through association. Food (UCS) associated with person who feeds (CS) produces pleasure (UCR and CR) = attachment bond.

Operant conditioning. Learning through reinforcement. Person who feeds the infant reduces discomfort from hunger and creates pleasure – both are reinforcing. Food is a *primary reinforcer*, person who feeds is *secondary reinforcer* and becomes a source of reward in his/her own right = attachment (Dollard and Miller, 1950).

EXPLANATION 2 The psychodynamic approach: Freud's theory (another cupboard love theory)

Infants have innate drive for pleasure (*pleasure principle*), motivates the id to seek oral satisfaction (focus of the infant's *libido*). Person providing satisfaction becomes love object = attachment.

EXPLANATION 3 The evolutionary approach: Bowlby's theory

- Attachment is adaptive and has been naturally selected, therefore infants born with a drive to become attached.
- Infants elicit caregiving through *social releasers*.
- Adults respond to social releasers. Sensitive responsiveness leads to a strong attachment (*caregiver sensitivity hypothesis*).
- Infants form one special relationship (*monotropy*) with the person who responds most sensitively.
- Leads to *internal working model*.
- Generates expectations about social relationships (*continuity hypothesis*).

RESEARCH related to Bowlby's theory

Study 1
HARLOW (1959)

Findings: Even the monkeys with contact comfort became quite maladjusted adults.

Conclusions: Underlines importance of interaction (sensitivity and responsiveness) in attachment.

Study 2
SROUFE ET AL. (1999)

Findings: Securely attached infants were rated highest in late childhood for social competence, were less isolated, more popular and more empathetic.

Conclusions: Demonstrates continuity.

PUTTING IT ALL TOGETHER

Research strongly suggests that quantity of care does not create strong attachments, thus supporting Bowlby's theory that attachment is innately driven and is related to quality of parenting. Strength of attachment may be affected by infant temperament rather than parenting.

EVALUATION

Strengths

1. Learning theory can explain attachment but food isn't only reinforcer, attention is too.

Limitations

1. Infants *not* most attached to the person who fed or spent most time with them (Schaffer and Emerson, 1964).

2. Monkeys became attached to contact-comfort 'mother', not the one with food (though this was non-human behaviour) (Harlow, 1959).

EVALUATION

Strengths

1. *Continuity hypothesis* supported by research (Hazan and Shaver, Sroufe *et al.*)

2. Supported by *monotropy* evidence (Schaffer and Emerson).

Limitations

1. *Temperament hypothesis* can also explain continuity (e.g. Belsky and Rovine).

2. Individual differences: some children with no early attachment have good adult relationships.

Cognitive psychology >
Developmental psychology >
Physiological psychology >
Individual differences >
Social psychology >
Research methods >

The development and
variety of attachments >
Deprivation and privation >
Critical issue: Day care >

Maternal deprivation hypothesis
Effects of deprivation/separation
Effects of privation

EXPLANATION of Bowlby's maternal deprivation hypothesis

1. Emotional care ('mother-love') is important for mental development, as important as good standard of physical care.

2. Children need a warm and continuous relationship with mother or 'permanent mother-substitute'.

3. Frequent and/or prolonged separations will disrupt continuity and lead to emotional disturbance.

4. *If* this happens before the age of *about* 2½ years (a *critical period*, though continuing risk up to age 5),

5. and if there is no substitute mother-person available.

KEY DEFINITION

Separation

- The physical absence of a primary caregiver but not necessarily of maternal care.

- The child may or may not receive suitable replacement care during the separation experience.

- If suitable care is provided then there is no *bond disruption* and separation need not have negative effects.

KEY DEFINITION

Deprivation

- The *loss* of care that is normally provided by a primary caregiver.

- More specifically *bond disruption* caused by repeated short-term separations or long-term separation, or can occur even in the presence of a caregiver.

- Bowlby suggested that this would have a detrimental effect on development.

starSTUDY on effects of deprivation

BOWLBY (1944)

Aims: To test the maternal deprivation hypothesis by looking at the past histories of emotionally maladjusted children – 'thieves' (lacking a social conscience) especially those diagnosed as *affectionless psychopaths*.

Procedures: Two groups of 44 children attending Bowlby's Child Guidance Clinic: experimental group were referred for thieving (14 were diagnosed as affectionless psychopaths), control group were experiencing emotional problems. Parents and children interviewed about infancy and childhood.

Findings: 86% of the affectionless thieves experienced frequent separations compared with 17% of the other thieves and 4% of the control group. 61% of all the thieves experienced no early separations compared with 96% of control group.

Conclusions: Suggests a link between early separation and lack of social conscience/affectionless psychopathy, i.e. lack of continuous care may cause emotional maladjustment.

Criticisms: (1) Data may be unreliable because retrospective and collected by Bowlby whose bias may have affected the interviews; **(2)** Only a correlation was demonstrated, therefore deprivation may not be a cause.

EVALUATION

Strengths

1. Emphasized importance of emotional care.

2. Had enormous impact on postwar thinking about childrearing and hospital care.

Limitations

1. *Critical period* challenged. Some studies of isolated children demonstrate good recovery despite many years of deprivation.

2. Could be privation rather than deprivation.

PUTTING IT ALL TOGETHER

Bowlby highlighted an important link between maternal care and healthy emotional development. He probably was wrong in some of the details, for example separation does not inevitably lead to deprivation, and deprivation may not be irreversible whereas privation may be.

Cognitive psychology	>	The development and variety of attachments	>	Maternal deprivation hypothesis
Developmental psychology	>			Effects of deprivation/separation
Physiological psychology	>	Deprivation and privation	>	Effects of privation
Individual differences	>	Critical issue: Day care	>	
Social psychology	>			
Research methods	>			

Deprivation

otherRESEARCH on effects of deprivation

Study 1
BOWLBY ET AL., 1956

Findings: TB children hospitalised under age 4 showed more maladjustment than 'normal' peers but not serious.

Conclusions: Suggests that dangers of maternal deprivation may have been overstated; early deprivation did not invariably cause emotional maladjustment. Perhaps some childen more securely attached and able to cope better.

Study 2
SKODAK AND SKEELS (1949)

Findings: Orphan children raised in home for mentally retarded (received care from other patients) IQs rose as compared with those who stayed in the orphanage.

Conclusions: Deprivation effects can be reversed when emotional care available.

Study 3
BOHMAN AND SIGVARDSSON (1979)

Findings: 26% of adopted children (total 600 Swedish adoptees) classified as problems at age 11; 10 years later same as normal children.

Conclusions: Deprivation effects can be reversed.

EFFECTS of deprivation

1. **Later maladjustment** e.g. Bowlby's 44 thieves developed *affectionless psychopathy*.

2. **Deprivation dwarfism** Hormones associated with emotional states stunt growth leading to underdevelopment (Gardner, 1972).

Separation

MODEL of effects of separation

The protest, despair, detachment (PDD) model (Robertson and Bowlby, 1952)

1. **Protest** immediate response, may last days.

2. **Despair** after distress subsides, child becomes hopeless, tearful.

3. **Detachment** within a week or so, apparent recovery but really giving up.

RESEARCH on effects of separation

Study 1
ROBERTSON AND BOWLBY (1952)

Findings: A two-year-old goes to hospital: Laura alternated between calm and distress.

Conclusions: Children who were thought to be settled were actually quite distressed; led to major social changes.

Study 2
ROBERTSON AND ROBERTSON (1968–73)

Findings: Jane, Lucy, Thomas and Kate all seemed to adjust well to foster care where substitute emotional care offered. John, who spent 9 days in a residential nursery (no substitute care), became very distressed and rejected mother's care.

Conclusions: Substitute emotional care can prevent *bond disruption* and prevent harmful effects of separation/deprivation.

⟳ PUTTING IT ALL TOGETHER

The effects of deprivation can be avoided if a child is given substitute emotional care. There are individual differences in the effects of separation/deprivation.

19

Cognitive psychology >	The development and variety of attachments >	Maternal deprivation hypothesis
Developmental psychology >		Effects of deprivation/separation
Physiological psychology >	Deprivation and privation >	**Effects of privation**
Individual differences >	Critical issue: Day care >	
Social psychology >		
Research methods >		

starSTUDY on effects of privation   HODGES AND TIZARD (1989)

Aims: To test the long-term effects of maternal deprivation/privation in institutional care, assessing the maternal deprivation (privation) hypothesis.

Procedures: Longitudinal study of 65 children placed in an institution when less than 4 months old who probably never formed any attachments. At age four, 24 had been adopted, 15 had returned to natural homes, the rest remained in the institution. Sample at age 16 was only 39 children. Data collected using questionnaires and interviewing children, parents, teachers.

Findings: At age 16: 'restored' group less likely to be closely attached than adopted children. All ex-institutional adolescents were less likely to have a special friend, to be part of a crowd, or to be liked by other children; more likely to be bullies.

Conclusions: Early privation had a negative effect on relationships when effort required from the child. Supports the maternal 'privation' hypothesis.

Criticisms: (1) Attrition: the final sample was possibly biased; **(2)** Adopted children might have been the 'nicer' ones in the first place and that's why they were selected for adoption.

KEY DEFINITION

Privation
- The *lack* of care that is normally provided by a primary caregiver, a contrast with deprivation which is the *loss* of such care.

- Like deprivation, lack of care can occur through physical separation or despite physical presence caregiver provides no emotional care (e.g. abuse).

- Consequences more severe than for deprivation.

EFFECTS of privation

1. **Cycle of privation** e.g. Quinton *et al.* (below).

2. **Reactive Attachment Disorder** Children develop protective emotional 'shell' and resist efforts to remove this shell. May permanently lack ability to have any lasting intimate relationships.

otherRESEARCH on effects of privation

Study 1
CURTISS (1977)

Findings: Genie was disinterested in other people and couldn't fully use language.

Conclusions: May be due to early emotional privation or physical privation or retardation.

Study 2
KOLUCHOVÁ (1991)

Findings: Czech twins did recover and marry after loving care from sisters.

Conclusions: Recovery past sensitive period (quality care after age 7) but they did have each other earlier.

Study 3
QUINTON ET AL. (1985)

Findings: Ex-institution women had extreme difficulties as parents e.g. lacking warmth and children in care.

Conclusions: May be lack of *internal working model* or may be having inadequate role models.

Study 4
RUTTER ET AL. (1998)

Findings: Romanian children adopted before age 2 have recovered.

Conclusion: Shows that recovery from extreme privation can be achieved given adequate care.

PUTTING IT ALL TOGETHER

Research generally suggests that, given the right kind of care, children can recover from early privation, but this recovery may only apply to certain relationships e.g. where the child is responding to a caring other.

Cognitive psychology >	The development and variety of attachments >	**Effects of day care**
Developmental psychology >		Effects on cognitive development
Physiological psychology >	Deprivation and privation >	Effects on social development
Individual differences >	**Critical issue: Day care >**	
Social psychology >		
Research methods >		

KEY DEFINITION

Day care

- A form of temporary care (i.e. not all day and night).

- Not by family members or someone well known to the child, usually outside the home.

- Thought to disrupt continuity of care between infant and main caregiver and lead to deprivation.

ARGUMENTS *against* day care

1. Separation and disruption of continuous care is harmful: derived from Bowlby's *maternal deprivation hypothesis*.

2. Quality of care offered in day care may not be as good as that given by parent e.g. lower quality and quantity of attention, more desire for peace and quiet. Howes and Hamilton (1992) found fewer secure attachments with caregivers.

3. Day care is related to negative outcomes. See evidence on pages 22 and 23.

ARGUMENTS *supporting* day care

1. Day care providers can provide lots of fun and provide stimulation

2. Mothers have to work and/or get bored at home. Brown and Harris (1978) found depression often related to being at home with children.

3. Secure attachment related to quality not quantity of care e.g. Schaffer and Emerson. Andersson (1992) found positive effects of high quality day care.

4. Day care is related to positive outcomes. See evidence on pages 22 and 23.

EVALUATION

of the arguments

1. **Individual differences.** Children who are shy (Pennebaker *et al.*, 1981) or whose mothers lack responsiveness (NICHD, 1997) do less well. Egeland and Hiester (1995) found insecurely attached children did best, possibly because they needed compensatory care whereas others don't.

2. **Number of hours.** NICHD (2001) found negative effects where day care more than 10 hours but other studies (e.g. Clarke-Stewart, 1994) have found no differences in attachment related to hours spent in day care (30 hours or more).

3. **Methodology of the studies.**

   - Often correlational, therefore can't say that day care is the *cause*.

   - So many variables involved makes it hard to produce a clear answer.

   - Many studies of day care were conducted in the 1980s, quality may have been poorer.

IMPROVING day care

1. **Consistency of care**. Low child-staff ratios related to more sensitive and positive interactions between caregiver and child (NICHD, 1999).

2. **Quality of care** can be improved. NICHD study found 23% of infant care providers give 'highly' sensitive infant care, 50% 'moderately' sensitive, 20% 'emotionally detached' from the infants.

PUTTING IT ALL TOGETHER

It's no wonder that views are divided for and against day care – because there are convincing arguments on both sides. Furthermore, factors such as individual differences and methodological flaws mean that research findings do not apply to all children.

21

Cognitive psychology >
Developmental psychology >
Physiological psychology >
Individual differences >
Social psychology >
Research methods >

The development and
variety of attachments >
Deprivation and privation >
Critical issue: Day care >

Effects of day care
Effects on cognitive development
Effects on social development

EXPLANATIONS of the effects of day care on cognitive development

1. **Stimulation** e.g. holding and interacting with infant creates more connections in the brain (Greenhough et al., 1987).

2. **Secure base** provided through secure attachment, facilitates exploration and thus cognitive development.

Cognitive development

- Changes in a person's mental structures, abilities and processes.

- This includes memory, perception, intelligence, creativity and so on.

- These changes occur over a person's lifespan.

Day care has NEGATIVE EFFECTS on cognitive development

Study 1
RUHM (2000)

Findings: Preschool children (4000 studied) tend to have lower verbal ability if mothers worked during child's first year; 5–6 year-olds tend to have worse reading and maths skills if mothers worked during

any of the child's first three years.

Conclusions: Day care has detrimental effect on scholastic skills.

Study 2
ERMISCH AND FRANCESCONI (2000)

Findings: Negative correlation between

child's educational attainment and how much the child's mother had been working when child was under 5.

Conclusions: Day care has detrimental effect on educational attainment.

Day care has POSITIVE EFFECTS on cognitive development

Study 1
ANDERSSON (1992)

Findings: In Sweden, school performance highest in children who started day care at age of 1 and lowest for those who did not have any day care.

Conclusions: Positive effects may be related to high quality of care.

Study 2
BURCHINAL ET AL. (2000)

Findings: African American children placed in high quality child care from 3 months had improved cognitive development, language development, and communication skills at age 3.

Conclusions: Day care may especially benefit low-income children.

Day care has NO EFFECTS on cognitive development

Study 1
HORWOOD AND FERGUSON (1999)

Findings: In New Zealand, marginally better cognitive performance (maths tests and reading tests) for children with working mothers.

Conclusions: Differences are marginal.

Study 2
HARVEY (1999)

Findings: Study involving 6000 children of working mothers; early cognitive delays had disappeared by age 12.

Conclusions: Effects not long lasting.

⟳ PUTTING IT ALL TOGETHER

It may be that children in day care receive less stimulation which will affect their cognitive development. On the other hand day care may be more stimulating than home care. Research findings support both possibilities.

Cognitive psychology >
Developmental psychology >
Physiological psychology >
Individual differences >
Social psychology >
Research methods >

The development and
variety of attachments >
Deprivation and privation >
Critical issue: Day care >

Effects of day care
Effects on cognitive development
Effects on social development

KEY DEFINITION

Social development

- The development of sociability, where child learns how to relate to others,

- And process of socialisation, in which child acquires knowledge and skills appropriate to his/her society.

- These changes occur over a person's lifespan.

EXPLANATIONS of the effects of day care on social development

1. **Attachment theory** Continuous care important for the *internal working model*, though good subsequent care may help.

2. **Interactions with other people** are increased in day care settings (children and adults), thus social development enhanced.

Day care has NEGATIVE EFFECTS on social development

Study 1
BELSKY AND ROVINE (1988)

Findings: Infants receiving more than 20 hours of day care per week under age 1 were more likely to be insecurely attached compared with children at home.

Conclusions: Early and long separation from mother affects attachment.

Study 2
NICHD REPORT (2001)

Findings: Children separated from their mothers for more than 10 hours a week early in life are more aggressive once they reach kindergarten, as rated by their mothers and by their teachers.

Conclusions: Day care experience may enhance anti-social behaviour.

Study 3
DiLALLA (1998)

Findings: Children who have little or no day care were more likely to behave prosocially.

Conclusions: Day care may inhibit socialisation.

Day care has NO EFFECTS on social development

Study 1
CLARKE-STEWART ET AL. (1994)

Findings: No difference in attachment security between children spending a lot of time in day care (30+ hours a week from age 3 months) with children who spent less time (10 hours or less).

Conclusions: Suggests that time spent away from mother not significant.

Day care has POSITIVE EFFECTS on social development

Study 1
SCHWEINHART ET AL. (1993)

Findings: Children in Headstart program had less delinquency and lower criminality at ages 14, 19 and 27 than control group.

Conclusions: Day care led to less anti-social behaviour in later life.

Study 2
CLARKE-STEWART ET AL. (1994)

Findings: Day care children coped better in social situations and negotiate better with peers.

Conclusions: Day care enhances social development (though causal link not shown).

Study 3
CREPS AND VERNON-FEAGANS (1999)

Findings: Infants starting day care before 6 months more sociable later than those starting later.

Conclusions: This suggests that early day care may be better for social development.

C PUTTING IT ALL TOGETHER

Children in day care experience more social contact which should further their social development – except possibly if they are insecure and/or shy. There are research findings to support both views.

Cognitive psychology	>	Stress as a bodily response >	**Bodily response to stressors**
Developmental psychology	>	Sources of stress	>
Physiological psychology	>	Critical issue: Stress	Stress and cardiovascular disorders
Individual differences	>	management	>
Social psychology	>		Stress and the immune system
Research methods	>		

EXPLANATIONS of the body's response to stressors

1. *Acute stress and the SAM system*: The immediate response to a stressor leads to arousal of the *sympathetic branch* of the *autonomic nervous system* (ANS) via the *hypothalamus*. This causes a 'fight or flight' response because the *adrenal medulla* produces *adrenaline*. Effects are sweatiness, and increased heart and breathing rate.

2. *Chronic stress and the HPA axis*: When stress continues the *hypothalamus* stimulates the *pituitary* to secrete ACTH which stimulates *adrenal glands* to produce *cortisol*. Cortisol helps maintain a steady supply of blood sugar for continued energy.

EXPLANATION of General Adaptation Syndrome (GAS)   (SELYE, 1936)

Stage 1: The alarm reaction stage Stressor recognised, adrenaline produced, 'fight or flight'.

Stage 2: Resistance stage Body adapts to persisting stressor and appears to be coping but resources gradually depleted.

Stage 3: Exhaustion stage Body can no longer maintain normal functioning. ANS symptoms reappear, adrenal gland damaged, immune system not coping, onset of stress-related illnesses.

EVALUATION of GAS

Strengths

1. Research support. Generated lots of research e.g. on stress and the immune system and cardiovascular disorders.

2. People without adrenal glands die without substitute hormones which shows physiological explanation is relevant to aspects of human behaviour.

Limitations

1. Exhaustion phase may not deplete resources, may increase e.g. cortisol and this blocks immune activity.

2. Not appropriate for human stress response because doesn't recognise cognitive influences. Model generated from research with non-human animals.

PUTTING IT ALL TOGETHER

When an animal is stressed a physiological response is produced. This differs depending on whether the stress is acute (SAM system) or chronic (HPA axis). The GAS model proposed that acute stress is adaptive but chronic stress results in depleted resources and physical illness.

KEY DEFINITION

Stress

- Subjective experience of a lack of fit between a person and their environment

- i.e. where the perceived demands of a situation are greater than a person's perceived ability to cope.

- Leads to a stress response as outlined on this page.

KEY DEFINITION

Stressor

- Any event that causes a stress reaction in the body.

- Stressors include environmental stressors (such as the workplace) and life events (such as illness or divorce).

- Various factors modify the effects of stressors such as individual differences and a sense of control.

NB the terms 'stress, 'stressor' and 'stress response' are used somewhat interchangeably.

Cognitive psychology >
Developmental psychology >
Physiological psychology >
Individual differences >
Social psychology >
Research methods >

Stress as a bodily response >
Sources of stress >
Critical issue: Stress management >

Bodily response to stressors

Stress and cardiovascular disorders

Stress and the immune system

Cardiovascular disorders

- Any disorder of the heart and circulatory system, such as
- *Hypertension* (high blood pressure), or
- *Coronary heart disease* (CHD) caused by atherosclerosis (the narrowing of the coronary arteries).

EFFECTS (of stress on cardiovascular disorders)

Stress directly increases

1. **Heart rate**, which may wear away the lining of the blood vessels.
2. **Blood pressure**, causes damage as high pressure would in any 'pipe'
3. **Glucose levels**, leading to clumps blocking the blood vessels (atherosclerosis).

starSTUDY on the effects of stress on cardiovascular disorders   KRANTZ ET AL. (1991)

Aims: To find out if mental stress could damage the heart (assessing *myocardial ischemia* – decreases the flow of blood to the heart). Also to see if CHD patients reacted differently to 'normal' patients.

Procedures: Participants performed 3 mildly stressful mental tasks (sums, Stroop test, public speaking). Measurements taken of participants' blood pressure and contraction of blood vessels (to measure ischemia).

Findings: Some cardiovascular patients had high levels of myocardial ischemia and increases in blood pressure during the mental tasks, but some patients had little or no ischemia/blood pressure increase. The control participants showed the lowest levels of both myocardial ischemia and blood pressure when performing the mental tasks.

Conclusions: Shows that mildly stressful cognitive tasks may cause CHD. However, there are individual differences as not all cardiovascular patients responded in the same way.

Criticisms: (1) Demonstrates a direct link unlike many other studies; **(2)** No record was made of patients' responses to activities involving no stress as a control, they may have had increased ischemia to other activities too, not just mild stress.

otherRESEARCH on the effects of stress on cardiovascular disorders

Study 1
WILLIAMS (2000)

Findings: 6 year follow up found that people who scored highest on anger scale were 2.69 times more likely to have a heart attack than those with lowest ratings.

Conclusions: Individuals prone to anger might benefit from anger management training.

Study 2
RUSSEK (1962)

Findings: CHD greatest among GPs and lowest in dermatologists.

Conclusions: Stress at least indirectly linked to CHD.

Study 3
ROZANSKI ET AL. (1999)

Findings: *Sympathetic branch* of the ANS more reactive in some individuals than others.

Conclusions: Hyperresponsive individuals may have more damage to cardiovascular system.

PUTTING IT ALL TOGETHER

Stress is clearly linked to cardiovascular disorders though this may be due to direct causes (e.g. increased heart rate) or indirect causes (e.g. increased alcohol intake which affects CHD). Individual differences are important.

Cognitive psychology >
Developmental psychology >
Physiological psychology >
Individual differences >
Social psychology >
Research methods >

Stress as a bodily response >
Sources of stress >
Critical issue: Stress management >

Bodily response to stressors
Stress and cardiovascular disorders
Stress and the immune system

star**STUDY** on the effects of stress on the immune system
KIECOLT-GLASER ET AL. (1995)

Aims: To demonstrate the direct effects of stress on the immune system by looking at how fast wounds healed in women experiencing high chronic levels of stress.

Procedures: Experimental group: 13 women caring for relatives with senile dementia, matched with control group. All participants given a wound, which was treated by a nurse; levels of *cytokines* were assessed to measure immune system activity, and questionnaire given to assess stress levels.

Findings: Complete wound healing took 24% longer in carers. Cytokine levels were higher in carers. Carers indicated they felt more stressed.

Conclusions: Shows that chronic stress depresses functioning of the immune system both in terms of healing and actual immune system activity.

Criticisms: (1) Important application to medical treatment; **(2)** Sample bias – married women – though they should have better immune functioning.

KEY DEFINITION

Immune system

- System of cells in the body concerned with fighting intruders such as viruses and bacteria.

- Creates a barrier to prevent foreign bodies (*antigens*) entering the body.

- Antigens that do enter are killed by white blood cells (*leucocytes*) and antibodies.

other**RESEARCH** on the effects of stress on the immune system

Study 1
COHEN ET AL. (1993)

Findings: Using viral-challenge found a positive correlation between levels of stress and the likelihood of catching a cold.

Conclusions: Suggests that stress makes illness more likely.

Study 2
RILEY (1981)

Findings: After 5 hours on a rotating turntable mice had a lowered lymphocyte count. After 3 days of 10 minutes rotation per hour mice implanted with cancer cells were more likely to develop tumours than control mice given no stress.

Conclusions: Stress causes susceptibility to tumours (use of control group permits causal conclusion).

Study 3
EVANS ET AL. (1994)

Findings: Students exposed to acute stress (public speaking) had increase in sIgA (an antibody), whereas levels of sIgA decreased during examination periods (chronic stress).

Conclusions: Suggests that stress has two effects on the immune system: up-regulation for very short-term acute stress and down-regulation for chronic stress.

EFFECTS of stress on the immune system

1. **GAS model** Stress leads to illness because body's resources (e.g. proteins for immune system) depleted.

2. **Cortisol directly suppresses the immune system** It decreases production of lymphocytes and antibodies.

other**RESEARCH** on stress and physical illness

Study 1   BRADY (1958)

Findings: Executive monkey (who had control over lever) died within a few weeks due to a perforated ulcer; yoked control unaffected despite equal exposure to shocks.

Conclusions: Stress not electric shocks causes ulcer. Presumably linked to immune system.

➤ PUTTING IT ALL TOGETHER

In the short term stress may enhance immune system activity but in the long term stress reduces immune system activity thus making an individual more susceptible to illness. The GAS model explains the link between stress and physical illness in a different way (resources are depleted).

Cognitive psychology >	Stress as a bodily response >	**Life changes**
Developmental psychology >	**Sources of stress** >	Workplace stressors
Physiological psychology >	Critical issue: Stress management >	Individual differences
Individual differences >		
Social psychology >		
Research methods >		

KEY DEFINITION

Life changes

- Events in a person's life that necessitate a significant adjustment.

- The adjustment or change requires psychic energy to be expended i.e. it is stressful.

- Examples include death of spouse, divorce, jail term, marriage, marital reconciliation.

WAYS in which life changes lead to stress

1. **Bereavement** Many of the changes involve loss. Effects strongest when loss is sudden and unexpected.

2. **Post-traumatic stress disorder** occurs after traumatic event involving real or potential grave physical harm.

starSTUDY on life changes as a source of stress
RAHE ET AL. (1970)

Aims: To test Holmes and Rahe's hypothesis that the number of life events experienced are positively correlated with illness, and to specifically look at a 'normal' population.

Procedures: SRRS completed by 2700 men aboard three US Navy Cruisers for previous 6 months, producing LCU (life change units) score. Record kept during tour of duty (6 months) to produce an illness score.

Findings: Significant, positive correlation (+0.118) between LCU and illness.

Conclusions: Supports link between life changes and physical illness.

Criticisms: (1) Recall of life events may be inaccurate; **(2)** SRRS may not be valid – focuses on acute events only and overlooks desirability and social resources.

otherRESEARCH on life changes as a source of stress

Study 1
JACOBS AND CHARLES (1980)

Findings: Children who developed cancer had families with a higher life change rating than a control group of children being treated for non-cancerous illnesses.

Conclusions: Increased life changes are a source of stress and greater ill health.

Study 2
STONE ET AL. (1987)

Findings: Improved reliability by asking participants to keep ongoing records and found that wherever there was an episode of illness there had been a significant increase in both undesirable and desirable events in the previous 4 days.

Conclusions: Stress does precede illness.

Study 3
DELONGIS ET AL. (1988)

Findings: Found a significant positive correlation of +0.59 between hassles and next-day illness.

Conclusions: Daily hassles may be a better predictor of stress.

other WAYS of measuring stress

1. **Daily hassles and uplifts scales:** De Longis et al. (1982) focused on strains of daily living rather than acute stress, plus uplifts.

2. **Perceived importance:** Moos and Swindle (1990) identified 8 areas of ongoing stress and assessed social resources = LISRES.

PUTTING IT ALL TOGETHER

Major life events involve change which reduces psychic energy thus predisposing an individual to become ill. However this can only explain some illness because major life events are relatively rare and not the only stressors we encounter.

Cognitive psychology >
Developmental psychology >
Physiological psychology >
Individual differences >
Social psychology >
Research methods >

Stress as a bodily response >
Sources of stress >
Critical issue: Stress management >

Life changes
Workplace stressors
Individual differences

KEY DEFINITION

Workplace stressors

- Some aspect of our working environment that we experience as stressful, and which causes a stress reaction in our body.

- Physical stressors such as noise, length of working day, and inherent danger.

- Psychosocial stressors such as work overload, role ambiguity or impending deadlines.

WAYS in which the workplace leads to stress

1. **Demand** Jobs high in demand/responsibility are stressful. Supported by Brady, Johansson et al., but not Marmot et al.

2. **Control** Jobs low in control are stressful. Supported by Marmot et al., Schaubroeck et al., Glass et al.

starSTUDY on workplace stressors as a source of stress
MARMOT ET AL. (1997)

Aims: To test *job-strain model* (stress due to high demand and low control).

Procedures: Over 7000 high grade (high job demand) and low grade (low job control) Civil Service employees (men and women) rated for cardiovascular disease, coronary risk factors, sense of job control, and amount of social support. Re-assessed 5 years later.

Findings: Higher grade civil servants developed fewest cardiovascular problems. Lower grade civil servants had weaker sense of job control and poorest social support. Cardiovascular disease also related to risk factors (smoking and being overweight).

Conclusions: Low control linked to higher stress and cardiovascular disorder, not fully supporting the job-strain model because high demand was not linked to illness.

Criticisms: (1) Can explain findings in terms of SES instead of control/demand; **(2)** Biased sample: urban, job-oriented and ambitious.

otherRESEARCH on workplace stressors as a source of stress

Study 1
JOHANSSON ET AL. (1978)

Findings: Sawyers in Swedish sawmill (high responsibility/demand) had more illness and higher levels of *adrenaline* than low risk group (e.g. maintenance workers with more job flexibility). Highest on work days rather than rest days.

Conclusions: Shows direct link between job demand, stress hormones and illness.

Study 2
SCHAUBROECK ET AL. (2001)

Findings: Some people had higher immune responses in low control situations.

Conclusions: Some people view negative work outcomes as being their fault. For these employees control can actually exacerbate the unhealthful effects of stress.

Study 3
GLASS ET AL. (1969)

Findings: Physical factor (noise) caused stress (measured by GSR) especially when unpredictable.

Conclusions: Lack of control is stressful.

PUTTING IT ALL TOGETHER

It appears difficult to identify what aspects of work are stressful. Some studies show that lack of control is stressful whereas other studies show that greater control/demand is stressful.

Cognitive psychology >	Stress as a bodily response >	Life changes
Developmental psychology >	Sources of stress	Workplace stressors
Physiological psychology >	Critical issue: Stress management >	**Individual differences**
Individual differences >		
Social psychology >		
Research methods >		

RESEARCH on the role of personality in modifying the effects of stressors

Type As are aggressive, ambitious, competitive leading to high blood pressure and hormone levels. Rosenman and Friedman (1959) assessed 3000 men and found 8½ years later twice as many Type As than Type Bs had died of cardiovascular problems. Type As also had higher blood pressure, cholesterol, lipoproteins and CHD.

Type Cs suppress negative emotions, unassertive, likeable, ignore own needs which has negative physiological consequences. Morris et al. (1981) found that women who had cancerous breast lumps showed less anger than women whose lumps were found to be non-cancerous.

Hardy personality Kobasa (1979) suggested that some people are more psychologically 'hardy' than others. Hardiness enables people to cope better with stress.

Direct link Depressed people who *thought* they had been given an anti-depressant had reduced sticky platelets (raised in depressed people and block arteries). Mood/personality may directly affect stress (Musselman, 2000).

RESEARCH on the role of culture in modifying the effects of stressors

Biological African-Americans may have higher blood pressure because ancestors travelled on slave ships where the ability to retain salt (e.g. to reduce diarrhea) would have had a selective advantage leading to natural selection of those who retain salt, and this retention leads to high blood pressure (Cooper et al., 1999).

Social Cooper et al. (1999) found hypertension (high blood pressure) rates highest in Africans living in urban societies; therefore seems to be social factors *but* Adams-Campbell et al. (1993) found greater hypertension in African-Americans even when social class (social factors) was controlled for.

Cognitive Racism, prejudice and negativity lead to increased stress – but then why don't women have more problems than men? Perhaps because women have greater social support.

Problems Very little research on ethnic minorities, stress scales based on mainstream stressors.

RESEARCH on the role of gender in modifying the effects of stressors

Biological Female hormone *oxytocin* reduces stress. When secreted in men the effects are reduced by male hormones. Women may have evolved a different stress response because they 'tend and befriend' when stressed rather than fight (Taylor et al., 2000).

Social Women have better social support networks and social support reduces stress (Kiecolt-Glaser et al., 1984); women engage in fewer unhealthy behaviours e.g. smoking and drinking.

Cognitive Females think differently about stress – they learn to suppress anger and have lower reactivity in stress situations; when males get angry blood pressure rises (Vögele et al., 1997).

Problems Some research suggests women have greater cardiovascular reactivity (Stone et al., 1989). Understanding of stress response largely based on male responses (gender biased).

PUTTING IT ALL TOGETHER

Individual differences (personality, culture and gender) can explain why life changes and workplace stressors affect people differently. Such differences may be biologically based or due to social and/or cognitive factors.

Cognitive psychology >
Developmental psychology >
Physiological psychology >
Individual differences >
Social psychology >
Research methods >

Stress as a bodily response >
Sources of stress >
Critical issue: Stress management >

Physiological methods
Psychological methods
Role of control

KEY DEFINITION

Stress management

- Different ways to cope with the negative effects of stress.

- May change the way our body responds to stress (the physiological approach).

- May change our relationship with the stressful situation (the psychological approach).

METHOD 1: Drug therapy

Benzodiazepines (BZs): Reduce CNS activity

Enhances GABA activity, a natural form of anxiety relief because it:

- Slows down nerve cell activity.

- Reduces *serotonin* which is arousing.

Beta-blockers: Reduce ANS activity

Reduce activity of *sympathetic nervous system* and associated undesirable symptoms e.g. increased cortisol.

EVALUATION

Strengths

1. Anxiolytic drugs work, as shown in trials with placebos (e.g. Kahn *et al.*, 1986).

2. Easy to use, little effort.

Weaknesses

1. Addiction, limit taking BZs to 4 weeks.

2. Treating symptoms rather than the problem.

KEY DEFINITION

Physiological approaches to stress management

- Techniques such as drugs and biofeedback.

- Designed to change the activity of the body's stress response system.

- Deals with the consequences of stress and not the causes.

METHOD 2: Biofeedback

Learning to control ANS/involuntary body activities:

- **Feedback.** Patient connected to a machine that provides information about ANS activity.

- **Relaxation.** Learn to control ANS.

- **Operant conditioning.** Successful behaviours are repeated because they are rewarding.

- **Transfer** to everyday situations.

Supported by Miller and DiCara (1967) who trained rats to increase/decrease heart rate.

EVALUATION

Strengths

1. Effective in treating behaviours (e.g. heart rate) and disorders (e.g. migraines).

2. No side effects.

Weaknesses

1. Requires expensive specialist equipment.

2. Treating symptoms and not problem.

3. Relaxation (a psychological method) alone reduces sympathetic activity.

⟳ PUTTING IT ALL TOGETHER

Drug therapy deals with the symptoms and not the causes of stress but sometimes that is all someone needs, and it's an easy way to deal with stress. Biofeedback requires more effort but may provide a longer term coping strategy in terms of relaxation.

Cognitive psychology	>	Stress as a bodily response	>	Physiological methods
Developmental psychology	>	Sources of stress	>	Psychological methods
Physiological psychology	>	Critical issue: Stress management	>	Role of control
Individual differences	>			
Social psychology	>			
Research methods	>			

METHOD 1: Stress inoculation training (SIT)

Meichenbaum's (1985) cognitive therapy aims to prepare (inoculate) an individual against stress.

1. **Conceptualisation phase**. Stress is a problem-to-be-solved. Break global stressors into specific components.
2. **Skills acquisition phase** (and rehearsal). Clients taught skills e.g. positive thinking, relaxation, using social support systems, time management.
3. **Application phase** (and follow through). Apply new coping skills in different situations using imagination, modelling, role play, training others.

RESEARCH on SIT

Study 1   **MEICHENBAUM (1977)**

Findings: SIT helped clients deal with target fear and a second, non-treated phobia more than systematic desensitisation did.

Study 2   **FONTANA ET AL. (1999)**

Findings: Students had lower heart rate and anxiety levels than controls after 6 week stress inoculation programme.

EVALUATION

Strengths

1. Effective.
2. Deals with causes not symptoms: now and in the future because focus on skills.

Weaknesses

1. Time-consuming, suitable for limited range of motivated individuals.
2. Unnecessarily complex, may be equally effective to be more positive and relax more.

KEY DEFINITION

Psychological approaches to stress management

- Techniques such as relaxation, hypnosis, or cognitive-behavioural methods.
- Coping achieved by altering the *perception* of the demands of a stressful situation.
- Deals with causes and long-term solutions rather than symptoms.

METHOD 2: Hardiness training

Kobasa (1979) suggested hardy individuals have 3 Cs: control, commitment and challenge (life changes are challenges to be overcome); all reduce ANS arousal to potential stressors.

Hardiness training involves:

1. **Focusing**. Recognise signs of stress e.g. muscle tension.
2. **Reliving stress encounters**. Analyse past situations.
3. **Self-improvement**. Insights lead to learning new techniques.

RESEARCH on hardiness

Study 1   **KOBASA (1979)**

Findings: 800 US executives with high stress/low illness scored high on three Cs; high stress/high illness group scored lower on these variables.

Study 2   **MADDI ET AL. (1998)**

Findings: Hardiness training more effective than relaxation and social support for 54 managers, resulted in decreasing self-reported strain and illness.

EVALUATION

Strengths

1. Effective
2. Deals with problem rather than symptoms.

Weaknesses

1. Research limited to middle-class executives. Control and challenge may be successful coping strategies for this group.
2. Is hardiness just being in control?

PUTTING IT ALL TOGETHER

Psychological methods of stress management have the advantage of providing long-term coping strategies for dealing with any stress that arises. However they have the disadvantage of requiring considerable effort – effort that may not be necessary when it may be equally effective just to relax more.

Cognitive psychology >
Developmental psychology >
Physiological psychology >
Individual differences >
Social psychology >
Research methods >

Stress as a bodily response >
Sources of stress >
Critical issue: Stress management >

Physiological methods
Psychological methods
Role of control

KEY DEFINITION

Control

- The extent to which an individual feels able to direct or regulate his/her behaviour.

- May feel controlled by other forces (internal or external) or may feel self-directed.

- Sense of perceived control may be more important than actual control.

EXPLANATIONS of the role of control related to stress

1. **Learned helplessness** (Seligman, 1975) occurs as a consequence of lack of perceived control. Supported by Glass et al. (1969): those participants given apparent control over noise were more persistent on an insoluble task. Breier et al. (1987) found that those in control actually had higher levels of adrenaline, evidence of greater ANS activity and stress.

2. **Locus of control** (Rotter, 1966) Moderates the perception of stress: internal locus means you feel responsible, external locus means you blame others. People with internal locus feel stress less and are less disrupted by it, e.g. Kim et al. (1997) found that children with an internal locus showed fewer signs of stress when parents divorced.

BUT **individual differences**: in some situations or for some people greater control may be distressing, e.g. Johansson et al. (1978) found highest stress levels in workers in a Swedish sawmill amongst those with greatest responsibility (see page 28).

RESEARCH on the role of control related to stress

Study 1
RODIN AND LANGER (1977)

Findings: Residents in nursing home with traditional care (all choices made for them) twice as likely to have died 18 months later than those given chance to make decisions about e.g. how their room was arranged and when they received visitors.

Conclusions: Suggests that perceived control may have major impact on health but this was a correlational study.

Study 2
COHEN ET AL. (1991)

Findings: Participants who felt their lives were unpredictable and uncontrollable were twice as likely to develop colds as those suffering low stress.

Conclusions: Lack of control associated with illness presumably because of higher stress.

Study 3
MARMOT ET AL. (1997)

Findings: Low control in civil servants linked to greater stress and more cardiovascular disorder.

Conclusions: Lack of control associated with higher stress and illness.

Study 4
WEISS (1972)

Findings: In a similar experiment to Brady (see page 26) found that the executive rat suffered fewer ulcers than the yoked control when knew whether the shock had actually been delivered.

Conclusions: Control alone not enough, need also to know that actions have been effective.

⟩ PUTTING IT ALL TOGETHER

Being able to regulate one's own behaviour can reduce the effects of stress though too much responsibility may increase stress.

Cognitive psychology
Developmental psychology
Physiological psychology
Individual differences
Social psychology
Research methods

Defining psychological abnormality

Biological and psychological models of abnormality

Critical issue:
Eating disorders

Definitions of abnormality

Limitations including cultural relativism

KEY DEFINITION

Abnormality

- A psychological condition or behaviour that departs (or deviates) from the norm.

- And/or is harmful and distressing to the individual or those around them.

- Abnormal behaviours are usually those that violate society's ideas of what is an appropriate level of functioning.

DEFINITION 1:
Statistical infrequency

- Abnormality is defined as behaviours that are extremely rare, i.e. statistically infrequent.

- Statistics are ways to summarise data. They can be used to define the 'norm' for any group of people, that is what is usual or regular or typical for any group.

- Normality is defined in terms of frequency, abnormality is defined in terms of infrequency or deviation from the norm.

DEFINITION 2:
Deviation from social norms

- Abnormal behaviour is seen as a deviation from implicit rules about how one 'ought' to behave. Anything that violates these rules is considered abnormal.

- Note that in this case deviation is from social rather than statistical norms.

- Social norms define what is undesirable. 'Desirability' is a standard set by a social group, i.e. 'social norms', such as seeing homosexuality as undesirable and therefore abnormal.

DEFINITION 3:
Failure to function adequately

- Mentally healthy people are judged as able to operate within certain acceptable limits, such as going to work, eating meals, and washing clothes.

- If any behaviour interferes with daily functioning, it may, according to these criteria, be considered abnormal.

DEFINITION 4:
Deviation from ideal mental health

- Abnormality is seen as deviating from an ideal of positive mental health, in a similar way to how physical illness is a deviation from signs of ideal physical health (body temperature, blood pressure, etc.).

- Jahoda (1958) listed signs of ideal mental health including a positive attitude towards the self, *self-actualisation*, resistance to stress and an accurate perception of reality.

⟲ PUTTING IT ALL TOGETHER

One way of defining abnormality is in terms of deviation – from statistical or social norms. The other way is concerned with healthy functioning – being able to function on a day-to-day basis (e.g. eating meals), or on a more global basis (e.g. self-actualisation).

Cognitive psychology >
Developmental psychology >
Physiological psychology >
Individual differences >
Social psychology >
Research methods >

Defining psychological
abnormality >
Biological and psychological
models of abnormality >
Critical issue:
Eating disorders >

Definitions of abnormality
Limitations including cultural
relativism

DEFINITION 1: Statistical infrequency

Limitations

1. Abnormal behaviour isn't always undesirable (e.g. genius); some undesirable behaviours are relatively common (e.g. depression).

2. Difficult to establish cut-off points, i.e. where abnormality begins and normality ends.

Strengths

Statistical criterion sometimes suitable e.g. for mental retardation.

Cultural relativism

Behaviours that are statistically infrequent in one culture may be statistically more frequent in another.

DEFINITION 2: Deviation from social norms

Limitations

1. Susceptible to abuse, e.g. homosexuality, Russian dissidents.
2. Judgments of deviance are related to context.

Strengths

Does distinguish between desirable and undesirable behaviour and does take into account the effect that behaviour has on others.

Cultural relativism

Social norms are defined by a dominant culture and then applied to other cultural groups.

DEFINITION 3: Failure to function adequately

Limitations

1. Who judges? A patient may be perfectly happy.
2. Dysfunctional behaviour may be functional for the patient.

Strengths

Does recognize subjective experience of the patient.

Cultural relativism

Definitions of adequate functioning are related to cultural ideas of how one's life should be lived.

DEFINITION 4: Deviation from ideal mental health

Limitations

1. Can anyone achieve these criteria?
2. Criteria for mental health are subjective, unlike physical health.

Strengths

A positive approach to the definition of abnormality because starts by defining health which is used as baseline for comparison.

Cultural relativism

Many criteria are culture-bound, e.g. *self-actualisation*, leading 'outsiders' to be diagnosed as abnormal.

KEY DEFINITION

Cultural relativism

- Behaviour cannot be judged properly unless viewed in cultural context.

- What is abnormal (i.e. norm violating) in one society may be perfectly normal (i.e. norm consistent) in another.

- This applies to subcultural groups as well – any group that shares rules, customs, morals and ways of interacting that bind the members together.

↻ PUTTING IT ALL TOGETHER

Each definition is problematic either for the individual being labelled abnormal or for society trying to find some objective means of identifying mental illness. All definitions are inevitably relative to cultural context.

Cognitive psychology >	Defining psychological abnormality >
Developmental psychology >	
Physiological psychology >	Biological and psychological models of abnormality >
Individual differences >	
Social psychology >	Critical issue: Eating disorders >
Research methods >	

The biological (medical) and psychodynamic models

The behavioural and cognitive models

ASSUMPTIONS of the biological (medical) model in relation to:

The causes of abnormality

1. Abnormality related to bodily states i.e. physical factors such as: genes, biochemistry, neuroanatomy and/or micro-organisms.

2. Abnormality inherited which can be demonstrated by looking at *concordance rates*. Certain genes lead to abnormal biochemistry (e.g. neurotransmitters, hormones) and/or abnormal neuroanatomy.

EVALUATION

1. Humane or inhumane? Patient not to blame but is placed in a passive role.

2. Cause or effect? Abnormal biochemistry may be either a cause of abnormality or an effect of becoming mentally ill.

3. Inconclusive evidence e.g. concordance rates of inherited disorder never 100%.

The treatment of abnormality

1. Treatment should be physical (somatic) e.g. using drugs or genetic testing.

2. Treatment should follow the medical model: identify symptoms → diagnose a syndrome → prescribe suitable treatment.

Examples: drugs, ECT (electro-convulsive therapy), psychosurgery.

EVALUATION

1. Treating symptoms and not necessarily causes may lead to *symptom substitution*.

2. Mental illnesses are not like physical illnesses, symptoms are frequently thoughts and feelings rather than somatic.

3. Ethical issue: lack of informed consent.

ASSUMPTIONS of the psychodynamic model in relation to:

The causes of abnormality

1. Mental disorder results from psychological rather than physical causes, and from early experiences.

2. Unresolved conflicts between id, ego and super-ego create anxiety and ego-defenses (e.g. repression) motivate unconscious behaviours.

EVALUATION

1. Very influential, Freud's concepts have become part of our culture.

2. Too much emphasis on sexual (physical) factors, too little on social factors.

3. Biased evidence, largely middle-class Viennese women suffering from neurosis.

The treatment of abnormality

1. If abnormal behaviour is the result of unconscious thoughts, then one must access such unconscious thoughts.

2. Treatment concerns the past because mental disorders had their origins there.

Examples: psychoanalysis, psychodrama.

EVALUATION

1. Present conflicts may be overlooked because focusing on the past.

2. Suitable for certain people e.g. YAVIS.

3. Not falsifiable. Psychoanalyst's interpretation cannot be proved wrong (denial is evidence of correctness).

℃ PUTTING IT ALL TOGETHER

The biological model suggests that mental illness is like physical illness leading to popular somatic therapies which, however, may prevent treating real psychological causes. The psychodynamic model may be outdated but many of its ideas have had a far-reaching influence.

Cognitive psychology	>	Defining psychological	The biological (medical) and
Developmental psychology	>	abnormality	>	psychodynamic models
Physiological psychology	>	Biological and psychological	The behavioural and cognitive
Individual differences	>	models of abnormality	>	models
Social psychology	>	Critical issue:	
Research methods	>	Eating disorders	>	

ASSUMPTIONS of the behavioural model in relation to:

The causes of abnormality

1. Abnormal behaviours are learned through *classical* and *operant conditioning*.

2. Only behaviour is important. Concepts of 'mental illness' and 'mind' are unnecessary.

3. The same laws apply to human and non-human animal behaviour.

The treatment of abnormality

1. Treatment should extinguish undesirable stimulus-response links and/or teach new ones.

2. Treatment should focus on symptoms not causes.

Examples: systematic desensitization (classical), token economy (operant), modelling (social learning theory).

EVALUATION

1. Scientific and testable model because experimental hypotheses can be easily generated.

2. Can account for some but not all human behaviour. The way we think does affect behaviour.

EVALUATION

1. Effective for a target range of behaviours i.e. those probably caused by conditioning e.g. phobias.

2. Treating the symptoms and not the cause, may result in *symptom substitution*.

3. Ethical issues: behavioural control, someone else determines appropriate goals for behaviour.

ASSUMPTIONS of the cognitive model in relation to:

The causes of abnormality

1. Abnormality is caused by faulty thinking. It is not the problem but the way you think about it that creates a problem.

2. The individual is in control; abnormality is faulty control.

The treatment of abnormality

1. Treatment should aim to change the way you think.

2. Treatment actively involves the client who must respond to challenges about faulty thinking.

Examples: stress inoculation therapy, Beck's cognitive triad.

EVALUATION

1. Faulty thinking may be the effect rather than the cause of a mental disorder.

2. Blames the patient not situational factors, and may overlook the latter, omitting this in explaining mental disorder.

EVALUATION

1. Effective and increasingly popular, offers long-term strategies for coping.

2. Lays blame and responsibility on patient. May not be suitable for some individuals.

⟳ PUTTING IT ALL TOGETHER

The behavioural model explains and offers appropriate treatment for certain 'target' mental illnesses. The cognitive model focuses on maladaptive thinking and provides long-term coping strategies.

		Anorexia and bulimia
Cognitive psychology >	Defining psychological abnormality >	Anorexia: Biological explanations
Developmental psychology >		Anorexia: Psychological explanations
Physiological psychology >	Biological and psychological models of abnormality >	Bulimia: Biological explanations
Individual differences >		Bulimia: Psychological explanations
Social psychology >	Critical issue:	
Research methods >	Eating disorders >	

KEY DEFINITION

Eating disorders

- Serious disruption of a person's eating habits or appetite.

- May reflect abnormal psychological functioning.

- The most common eating disorders are anorexia nervosa and bulimia nervosa.

KEY DEFINITION

Anorexia nervosa

- Seriously underweight which is denied.

- Continued self-starvation because of *fear* of becoming obese.

- Obsessive eating habits and exercise.

CLINICAL CHARACTERISTICS
of anorexia nervosa

1. *Anxiety*, not simply obsessed with weight but fearful of weight gain.

2. *Weight* loss considered abnormal when it drops below 85% of the individual's normal weight, based on age and height. People with anorexia develop unusual eating habits, may repeatedly check their body weight, and engage in compulsive exercise.

3. *Body-image distortion*, inability to see own thinness, denial of seriousness of condition.

4. *Amenorrhoea* more than three months. Other physical symptoms, e.g. paleness, hair falling out.

KEY DEFINITION

Bulimia nervosa

- Person habitually engages in uncontrollable eating (known as bingeing),

- Followed by self-induced vomiting or other compensatory behaviours (purging).

- Abnormal concern with body size and a morbid fear of being or becoming fat.

CLINICAL CHARACTERISTICS
of bulimia nervosa

1. *Binge*. Eat excessive amounts and then feel guilty and self-disgusted

2. *Purge* to compensate for overindulgence and prevent weight gain. May lead to feeling ashamed.

3. *Frequency* binge–purge at least twice a week for 3 months.

4. *Body image* and self-esteem unduly influenced by body shape and weight, inappropriate perception of own body.

5. *Contrast with anorexia*: not outside normal range of weight for age/height, but similar fear of gaining weight and intense dissatisfaction with body.

DIFFERENCES between anorexia nervosa and bulimia nervosa

Anorexia nervosa (restricting type)	Bulimia nervosa
Severely underweight	Slightly underweight or near normal weight
Not hungry	Intense hunger
Purge to maintain low weight	Purge to compensate for overeating
Less antisocial behaviour	Tends to antisocial behaviour and alcohol abuse
Amenorrhoea	Amenorrhoea only if weight loss extreme
More immature	More mature
Likely to reject the feminine role	More likely to be sexually active
More likely to have been compliant towards family pre-disorder	More likely to have been in conflict with family pre-disorder

PUTTING IT ALL TOGETHER

The key differences between anorexia and bulimia are related to fear of becoming fat (anorexia) versus self-disgust with eating too much (bulimia), being perfectionist versus impulsive and resisting food versus overeating.

Cognitive psychology >	Defining psychological abnormality >	Anorexia and bulimia
Developmental psychology >		**Anorexia: Biological explanations**
Physiological psychology >	Biological and psychological models of abnormality >	Anorexia: Psychological explanations
Individual differences >		Bulimia: Biological explanations
Social psychology >	Critical issue: Eating disorders >	Bulimia: Psychological explanations
Research methods >		

starSTUDY on biological explanations of anorexia nervosa

HOLLAND ET AL. (1988)

Aims: Compare concordance rates in MZ and DZ twins to find support for genetic cause.

Procedures: 25 MZ and 20 DZ female twins interviewed where at least one twin had had anorexia. Questions asked about body mass, length of amenorrhea, drive to be thin, body dissatisfaction and incidence in relatives.

Findings: 25 (56%) of MZ twins concordant for anorexia, 1 (5%) of DZ twins were. Greater similarity for MZ twins in amenorrhea, drive to be thin, and body dissatisfaction.

Conclusions: Heritability may be as high as 80%. Factors such as drive to be thin also genetic because closer in MZ than DZ.

Criticisms: (1) Diagnosis of anorexia not always correct so may be a predisposition to development of mental disorder/eating disorder not anorexia specifically; **(2)** MZ twins may be treated more similarly than DZ twins, therefore environmental causes.

Biological EXPLANATIONS

EXPLANATION 1: Genetic factors

Aspects of physiological functioning may be inherited. These include:

1. Abnormal neurotransmitter levels (e.g. *serotonin*).
2. Abnormal development of the *hypothalamus*.
3. Obsessive personality produces perfectionist behaviour (Klump *et al.*, 2000).

EXPLANATION 2: Neuroanatomy

1. **Malfunction of hypothalamus:** controls serotonin, emotion, and hunger. LH produces feelings of hunger, VMH suppresses hunger. Damaged LH leads to no feelings of hunger, VMH continues to send signals to suppress hunger.
2. **Malfunction of hippocampus:** increased *cortisol* reduces functioning of hippocampus further increasing levels of cortisol, explains vicious cycle.

EXPLANATION 3: Biochemical factors

1. **Increased serotonin** in the brain associated with suppressed appetite and increased anxiety and obsessive behaviour. Starvation lowers *tryptophan* which is needed to manufacture serotonin.
2. **Adrenaline and cortisol** (increased through stress) reduce appetite.
3. **Biochemical factors** change as a result of starvation: Fichter and Pirke (1995) (*starvation hypothesis*).

PUTTING IT ALL TOGETHER

Genetic studies show a strong inherited component. Abnormal neuroanatomy (e.g. damaged LH) and/or biochemical factors (e.g. increased serotonin) may be caused by genetic factors or could be effects of the illness.

EVALUATION

Strengths
1. Evidence to support biological basis.
2. Can lead to successful drug therapies e.g. antidepressants (reduce serotonin).

Limitations
1. Research often involves very small samples.
2. No one sole biological mechanism found.
3. Biological explanations cannot account for recent increase in anorexia.
4. Nor explain why not 100% concordance in twins.

Diathesis-stress model. Some individuals are born with a biological predisposition to develop anorexia; disorder then triggered by life stressors. Biological mechanisms may perpetuate the illness.

Cognitive psychology >	Defining psychological	Anorexia and bulimia
Developmental psychology >	abnormality >	Anorexia: Biological explanations
Physiological psychology >	Biological and psychological	**Anorexia: Psychological explanations**
Individual differences >	models of abnormality >	Bulimia: Biological explanations
Social psychology >	Critical issue:	Bulimia: Psychological explanations
Research methods >	Eating disorders >	

starSTUDY on psychological explanations of anorexia nervosa

BECKER ET AL. (2000)

Aims: To use a naturally-occuring situation where television introduced to Fiji to see effects this would have on attitudes and incidence of anorexia.

Procedures: Before TV introduced 63 native Fijian girls questioned about eating habits. Three years later, a further sample of 65 girls (average age 17) questioned about views on eating and television.

Findings: Number who said they vomited to control weight had risen from 3% to 15%. Number at risk of disordered eating had risen from 13% to 29%. Those who reported watching most TV more likely to be at risk.

Conclusions: Suggests that media exposure to Western methods of weight control and ideals of thinness leads to changed attitudes towards eating.

Criticisms: (1) Findings do not necessarily demonstrate a cause because it is a natural experiment;
(2) Changed attitudes may not lead to eating disorders.

Psychological EXPLANATIONS

EXPLANATION 1: The Psychodynamic approach

Bruch (1980): poor parenting and a struggle for autonomy. Mother doesn't cope with her infant's needs, leading child to feel ineffectual. In adolescence, anorexia is a means of exerting self-control and establishing independence. Mother's continuing relationship problems mean a desire on the mother's part to retain dependence and encourage immaturity.

EVALUATION

1. Bruch's explanation based on extensive case histories.
2. But difficult to falsify (prove wrong).

EXPLANATION 2: The Behavioural approach

1. **Classical conditioning:** An association between thinness and admiration is learned.

2. **Operant conditioning:** Continuing admiration is reinforcing; more weight loss more admiration. Also negative reinforcement – escaping from an undesirable situation.

3. **Vicarious reinforcement:** slimness ideal is learned through the media. We learn what behaviours are successful (being thin) and may imitate this behaviour under appropriate conditions.

EVALUATION

1. Explains gender differences.
2. Explains cultural differences: Anorexia rare in other cultures (e.g. Sui-Wah, 1989). Though other evidence of universal rates (Hoek et al., 1998).
3. Doesn't explain individual differences: exposure to thin models doesn't always lead to anorexia.

EXPLANATION 3: The Cognitive approach

Faulty cognitions ('I am unattractive and overweight') lead to excessive dieting. Inability to control dieting even though it is life threatening is an example of a maladaptive way of thinking.

EVALUATION

1. Can explain individual differences: Only those with faulty cognitions are affected by thin models.
2. Distorted cognitions may be *effect not cause*.
3. Has led to successful cognitive therapies. Desire to become thin (faulty cognition) should be focus of therapy no matter what the cause.

⟳ PUTTING IT ALL TOGETHER

Individuals born with a genetic predisposition for anorexia (diathesis) may develop the illness if exposed to certain psychological factors ('stress'). No one psychological explanation is right but each may contribute to aspects of the illness.

Cognitive psychology	>	Defining psychological abnormality	>	Anorexia and bulimia
Developmental psychology	>			Anorexia: Biological explanations
Physiological psychology	>	Biological and psychological models of abnormality	>	Anorexia: Psychological explanations
Individual differences	**>**			**Bulimia: Biological explanations**
Social psychology	>	Critical issue:		Bulimia: Psychological explanations
Research methods	>	Eating disorders	>	

starSTUDY on biological explanations of bulimia nervosa

KENDLER ET AL. (1991)

Aims: Compare concordance rates in MZ and DZ twins to find support for genetic cause.

Procedures: 1000 twin pairs (Virginia twin registry) interviewed. Same interviewer never interviewed both twins.

Findings: In MZ twins there was 26% concordance and 16% for DZ twins. Most bulimics also reported other mental disorders at some time including anorexia (10% of them), depression (51%), phobia (42%).

Conclusions: Bulimia has a strong genetic component, but less than for anorexia, heritability may be as high as 55%. Relationship between bulimia and other mental disorders suggests a general vulnerability for mental illness.

Criticisms: (1) Lack of consistent findings due to unreliable diagnosis (e.g. Bulik *et al.* (2000) found 83% heritability for bulimia and 58% for anorexia); **(2)** Twins may not be representative of general population, may be more prone to mental illness than non-twins.

Biological EXPLANATIONS

EXPLANATION 1: Genetic factors

Aspects of physiological functioning may be inherited. These include:

1. Abnormal neurotransmitter levels (e.g. *serotonin*, CCK).

2. Abnormal development of the *hypothalamus*.

3. Impulsive personality (Lilenfield *et al.*, 2000).

EXPLANATION 2: Neuroanatomy

1. **Malfunction of hypothalamus:** controls *serotonin*. LH produces feelings of hunger, VMH suppresses hunger. Damaged VMH leads to no feelings of fullness and low levels of serotonin stimulate LH leading to more hunger (anorexia linked to damaged LH).

EXPLANATION 3: Biochemical factors

1. **Decreased serotonin** in the brain leads to enhanced appetite and overeating (followed by guilt) (Galla, 1995). Bulimics often have carbohydrate craving which enhances *serotonin* production (Turner *et al.*, 1991). Serotonin either predisposes an individual to develop bulimia, and/or perpetuates the disorder.

2. **Decreased CCK** (*cholecystokinin*) (Kissileff *et al.*, 1996). CCK normally leads to feelings of fullness.

PUTTING IT ALL TOGETHER

Individuals are probably predisposed genetically to develop bulimia but less so than for anorexia. Genes may cause abnormal neuroanatomy (damaged VMH) and/or biochemistry (decreased serotonin).

EVALUATION

Strengths

1. Evidence to support biological basis.

2. Stereotypical set of characteristics suggests biological vulnerability.

3. Successful drug therapies e.g. SSRIs.

Limitations

1. Lack of consistency in findings.

2. No one sole biological mechanism has been found.

3. Biological explanations cannot account for fact that bulimia has increased in past 30 years.

4. Nor explain why there is not 100% concordance for bulimia in twins.

Cognitive psychology >	Defining psychological abnormality >	Anorexia and bulimia
Developmental psychology >		Anorexia: Biological explanations
Physiological psychology >	Biological and psychological models of abnormality >	Anorexia: Psychological explanations
Individual differences >		Bulimia: Biological explanations
Social psychology >	Critical issue: Eating disorders >	**Bulimia: Psychological explanations**
Research methods >		

starSTUDY on psychological explanations of bulimia nervosa
CUTTS AND BARRIOS (1986)

Aims: To investigate the cognitive explanation of bulimia, looking at fear of weight gain.

Procedures: Thirty females (18–25) assigned to bulimic or control group on basis of questionnaire. Given description of a neutral scene (in a library) and one about weight gain; asked to imagine themselves in these situations.

Findings: Both groups showed similar responses to neutral scene but bulimics had higher physiological activity when imagining weight gain and greater subjective distress.

Conclusions: Supports view that fear of weight gain may be a factor in bulimia. Faulty perceptions could trigger biological responses and/or behavioural cycle of reinforcement.

Criticisms: (1) Suggests a form of treatment – cognitive therapy; **(2)** May be extraneous variables e.g. some personality characteristics co-vary with faulty perceptions.

Psychological EXPLANATIONS

EXPLANATION 1: The Psychodynamic approach

1. **Childhood abuse:** Bulimia is a means of punishing the body, and expressing self-disgust. McLelland *et al.* (1991) found that 30% of patients with eating disorders had reported abuse in childhood.

2. **Bulimia may represent conflicting wishes** for merger and autonomy. Bingeing is merging with engulfing maternal object; terror of engulfment results in purging (Chassler, 1998).

EVALUATION

1. Not all bulimics have been abused, nor are merger and autonomy always issues.

2. May distract from other explanations.

EXPLANATION 2: The Behavioural approach

1. **Direct conditioning:** Indulgence (bingeing) and guilt relief (purging) are rewarding.

2. **Indirect conditioning:** Bulimics imitate mothers and/or media; also learn specific behaviours through imitation (e.g. how to purge).

3. **Cultural factors:** Nasser (1986) found that Arab female students in London twice as likely to express abnormal attitudes about eating than those in Cairo.

EVALUATION

1. Nasser's finding may be due to differences between students who choose to study abroad and those who stay at home.

2. Mumford et al. (1991) found most traditional Asian girls in UK more likely to be bulimic – perhaps because they experience greater conflict and stress.

EXPLANATION 3: The Cognitive approach

1. **The disinhibition hypothesis** (Ruderman, 1986): 'restrained' eaters deal with overeating by losing sense of self-restraint which leads to disinhibited behaviour.

2. **Distorted body image** leads to greater desire for weight loss.

EVALUATION

1. Disinhibition hypothesis supported by Herman and Mack (1975), unrestrained eaters did eat more after 'pre-load'.

2. Support for cognitive factors from Cutts and Barrios (above).

3. Distorted thinking may not be a cause; it may be a consequence of an eating disorder.

 PUTTING IT ALL TOGETHER

No one psychological explanation explains all aspects of the disorder or the disorder in all individuals but psychological explanations can account for cultural differences.

Cognitive psychology	>
Developmental psychology	>
Physiological psychology	>
Individual differences	>
Social psychology	>
Research methods	>

Conformity and minority influence	>
Obedience	>
Critical issue: Ethical issues	>

Majority influence (conformity)
Minority influence

KEY DEFINITIONS

Social influence

- How thoughts and behaviour of individuals are influenced by others.
- Others may be actual or imagined.
- For example, majority and minority influence and obedience.

Majority influence (conformity)

- Form of social influence resulting from exposure to majority.
- Tendency to adopt behaviour and/or attitudes of reference group.
- More likely to influence public behaviour than private attitudes.

EXPLANATIONS of why people yield to majority influence (i.e. conform)

1. **Normative influence**. Compliance to group behaviour without change of opinion.
2. **Informational influence**. Conforming because majority seen as being right. Likely in ambiguous situations. More likely to lead to change of opinion.

FACTORS that affect majority influence

1. **Size of the majority**. A majority of 3 is sufficient to influence one person.
2. **Cultural factors**. Majority influence is more pronounced in *collectivist* societies.

starSTUDY on majority influence   AScH (1956)

Aims: To find out how people would behave on an unambiguous task, whether they would be influenced by the behaviour of others, or would stick to what they knew to be right.

Procedures: 123 male American undergraduates tested individually in groups of confederates, each asked to state whether 'standard' line same as other 3 lines. Confederates told to give same incorrect answer on 12 critical trials out of 18. True participant was always the last or last but one to answer.

Findings: On critical trials, 36.8% of responses by true participants conformed to unanimous confederates. 25% of participants never gave a wrong answer; 75% conformed at least once. 1% gave wrong answers when no confederates.

Conclusions: Shows conformity to group pressures even when answer is clear. Also evidence of independent behaviour (resisting group pressure) on two-thirds of the trials.

Criticisms: (1) Performance on an insignificant task may not generalize to real life; **(2)** The study may be 'a child of its time' (Perrin and Spencer, 1980), the era of McCarthyism.

otherRESEARCH on majority influence (conformity)

Study 1   SHERIF (1935)

Findings: When stimulus is ambiguous participants' estimates of how far a point of light appears to move (autokinetic effect) is affected by group norms.

Conclusions: Shows tendency to establish and conform to group norms.

Study 2   SCHACHTER (1951)

Findings: Participants less likely to elect to work with confederates who disagreed with views of how to treat a delinquent (Johnny Rocco).

Conclusions: Supports view that fear of rejection/ridicule is reason for conforming to group.

Study 3   BURGER AND COOPER (1981)

Participants high in personal control less conformist.

Study 4   EAGLY AND CARLI (1981)

Women more conformist than men.

PUTTING IT ALL TOGETHER

People conform in ambiguous situations because they aren't sure (informational influence) and conform when in the company of new people to be liked (normative influence). There are individual differences in the extent to which people conform (e.g. gender or self-confidence).

Cognitive psychology >
Developmental psychology >
Physiological psychology >
Individual differences >
Social psychology >
Research methods >

Conformity and minority influence >
Obedience >
Critical issue: Ethical issues >

Majority influence (conformity)
Minority influence

KEY DEFINITION

Minority influence

- Form of social influence where people reject the established norm of the majority of group members.
- Individuals are converted to the position of the minority.
- Likely to change private opinion rather than just public behaviour.

Majority versus minority influence

Majority ⟶ establishes norms ⟶ compliance

Minority ⟶ challenges beliefs, leading to reappraisal ⟶ conversion

EXPLANATIONS of why people yield to minority influence

1. **Group identification**. Minority influence greater when coming from members of our ingroup (e.g. Maass *et al.*, 1982).
2. **Social cryptoamnesia** (Perez *et al.*, 1995). Attitude change gradual until it becomes the 'zeitgeist'. Then *snowball effect* (van Avermart, 1996).

FACTORS that affect minority influence

1. **Size of minority**. One may be more influential than two.
2. **Size of majority**. Minority doesn't affect majority of more than 4 (*social impact model* and Clark and Maas below).
3. **Behavioural style**. Consistency, flexibility and confidence.

starSTUDY on minority influence

MOSCOVICI ET AL. (1969)

Aims: To see if a consistent minority causes participants to change their views in an unambiguous situation.

Procedures: 32 groups of 6 females (2 confederates) shown 36 blue slides. Confederates consistently said slides were green. In a second experiment, participants did same task and reported answers individually. In a third experiment, confederates were inconsistent.

Findings: (1) Participants agreed with the minority on 8.42% of the trials. 32% gave the same answer as the minority at least once. (2) Greater agreement with confederates in private. (3) When the confederates were inconsistent, agreement with the minority was reduced to 1.25%.

Conclusions: Minorities can influence majority opinion to a small degree. Minority has greater influence on private opinion. Consistency is important.

Criticisms: (1) Biased and atypical sample: female undergraduates and majority of 4; (2) Flexibility of minority may be more important than consistency (see Nemeth and Brilmayer).

otherRESEARCH on minority influence

Study 1   **CLARK (1994)**

Findings: Students who were told the outcome of *Twelve Angry Men* more likely to shift their opinions than those who just read film transcript.

Conclusions: Shows effects of minority influence (reading arguments) and majority influence (hearing how others behaved).

Study 2   **NEMETH AND BRILMAYER (1987)**

Findings: Minority who refused to change opinion in mock-jury had no effect on others.

Conclusions: Flexibility important.

Study 3   **CLARK AND MAASS (1960)**

Findings: Minority effect only when majority group = 4 (with a minority of one), not when majority = 8 or 12.

Conclusions: Size of *majority* matters.

PUTTING IT ALL TOGETHER

Minority influence explains how opinions rather than behaviour change (innovation). Behavioural style (consistency, flexibility) matters as does the size of the minority and the size of the majority.

Cognitive psychology >
Developmental psychology >
Physiological psychology >
Individual differences >
Social psychology >
Research methods >

Conformity and minority influence >
Obedience >
Critical issue: Ethical issues >

Obedience to authority
Resistance to obedience
Validity

KEY DEFINITION

Obedience to authority

- Form of social influence.

- Person acts in response to direct order from perceived authority.

- Implication that person wouldn't otherwise have responded in this way.

FACTORS that influence obedience to authority

1. **Proximity of victim**. Obedience drops as proximity increases (Milgram found 40%).

2. **Proximity of authority**. Obedience decreases as proximity decreases (Milgram found 21% obedience).

3. **Presence of allies**. Obedience decreases with disobedient allies (Milgram found 10% obedience).

EXPLANATIONS of psychological processes in why people obey

1. **Gradual commitment** means it is difficult to subsequently change mind.

2. **Agentic shift**. Person sees themselves as agent carrying out another's wishes. Shift from *autonomous* to *agentic* state.

3. **Role of buffers** protect person from consequences.

star**STUDY** on obedience to authority   MILGRAM (1963)

Aims: To investigate whether ordinary people (not just German soldiers) will obey a legitimate authority even when required to injure another person – i.e. obedience to unjust authority.

Procedures: 40 male volunteers given role of 'teacher' and asked to administer shocks to 'learner' (confederate). As shocks increased teacher encouraged to continue despite pre-arranged objections from learner. Participants told at start they were free to leave.

Findings: Psychology students estimated less than 3% would go to the maximum level (450 volts). In fact 65% of participants continued to maximum. Only 5 participants (12.5%) stopped at 300 volts, the point when the learner first objected.

Conclusions: Ordinary people are obedient to unjust authority, so it is not evil people who commit evil crimes but ordinary people who are just obeying orders, a situational rather than dispositional explanation for obedience.

Criticisms: **(1)** *Demand characteristics* may have led to unnaturally high obedience e.g. prestigious University setting. **(2)** Individual differences – not everyone was obedient.

other**RESEARCH** on obedience to authority

Study 1   HOFLING ET AL. (1966)

Findings: 21 out of 22 nurses obeyed instructions from unknown doctor over phone for unknown drug (Astroten). Said afterwards they obeyed because expected to obey doctors.

Conclusions: Obedience does occur in real life situations, though Rank and Jacobsen (1975) found nurses less obedient when allowed to discuss action and drug was known (Valium).

Study 2   BICKMAN (1974)

Findings: Pedestrians more likely to obey man in uniform.

Conclusions: People more likely to obey someone who appears to be in authority.

Study 3   MEEUS AND RAAJMAKERS (1995)

Findings: 22 out of 24 interviewers continued pressure even when interviewees complained.

Conclusions: High obedience in face-to-face setting.

PUTTING IT ALL TOGETHER

Obedience is explained in terms of situational factors (e.g. proximity of victim or authority) or psychological factors (e.g. agentic shift, buffers). It could also be explained by dispositional factors (some people born to be more obedient).

Cognitive psychology >
Developmental psychology >
Physiological psychology >
Individual differences >
Social psychology >
Research methods >

Conformity and minority influence >
Obedience >
Critical issue: Ethical issues >

Obedience to authority
Resistance to obedience
Validity

EXPLANATIONS of how people might resist obedience

1. **Situational factors**: proximity of victim/authority figure, presence of allies.

2. **Psychological processes**: *autonomous state* (sense of personal responsibility and awareness of consequences), personality, past experience (leads to awareness of consequences), lack of gradual commitment, role of buffers.

RESEARCH on resistance to obedience

Study 1
MILGRAM (1974)

Findings: Interviews with participants showed reasons for resistance e.g. Gretchen Brandt spent youth in Nazi Germany and was aware of consequences of obedience; Jan Rensaleer was an electrical engineer and knew what shocks could do; minister had strong sense of moral responsibility.

Conclusions: Some people have personal characteristics and/or knowledge that enable them to resist.

Study 2
GAMSON ET AL. (1982)

Findings: 76% of groups disobeyed pressure to sign affidavit giving MHRC permission to their opinions in a trial.

Conclusions: Once sufficient group members make a stand, whole group will conform – resistance to authority as a result of minority and majority influence.

Study 3
VENKATESAN (1966)

Findings: True participant (last to register an opinion) conformed to majority opinion except when most of the confederates made statements strongly favouring one suit.

Conclusions: When individuals feel forced to conform they may react by asserting their independence.

Extra STUDY on conformity and obedience
ZIMBARDO ET AL. (1973)

Aims: To investigate conformity to social roles, to see whether anti-social behaviour is situational or dispositional.

Procedures: 21 volunteers randomly given role as prisoner or guard. Clothing and procedures led to deindividuation.

Findings: Guards became tyrannical, prisoners surprisingly obedient despite harsh treatment. Study stopped after 6 days.

Conclusions: Prison behaviour explained by situational factors (conformity/compliance to social roles).

Criticisms: (1) *Demand characteristics* – behaved like they thought they should from seeing films of prison life. (2) Lacked usefulness – didn't change prison system.

The obedience alibi   MANDEL (1998)

Findings: Officers of Reserve Police Battalion 101 in Poland in World War II obeyed order to kill Jews despite close proximity, absence of authority figure and presence of disobedient peers.

Conclusions: Other factors influence obedience in real life. Milgram's obedience research simply offered an 'alibi' for murder during the holocaust.

PUTTING IT ALL TOGETHER

The same factors that explain high obedience can be reversed to explain resistance to obedience. This suggests that people are not controlled by situational factors and can exert their own will.

Cognitive psychology	>	Conformity and minority influence		Obedience to authority
Developmental psychology	>		>	Resistance to obedience
Physiological psychology	>	Obedience	>	Validity
Individual differences	>	Critical issue: Ethical issues	>	
Social psychology	>			
Research methods	>			

KEY DEFINITION

Validity

- Refers to the legitimacy of a study.

- The extent to which the findings can be applied to real-life.

- Either as a consequence of internal or external validity.

KEY DEFINITION

Experimental validity

- Concerns the validity of *experiments*.

- How they are carried out, what conclusions are drawn, and implications for understanding related aspects of real life.

- Affected by threats to internal and external validity.

KEY DEFINITION

Internal validity

- Concerns what is going on inside a study.

- High if observed effect can be attributed to the experimental manipulation rather than some other factor (*confounding variable*).

- Low internal validity may lead to wrong conclusion.

KEY DEFINITION

External validity

- Concerns what is beyond specific situation studied.

- For example, being able to generalize findings to other people (*population validity*)

- And/or other settings (*ecological validity*).

EXAMPLES of low internal validity in social influence research

- Orne and Holland (1968) claimed Milgram's participants knew no-one is harmed in an experiment. Therefore participants obeyed whereas they wouldn't in real life, so experiment not testing what it claimed to test.

- Holland (1967) replicated the experiment and afterwards 75% said they didn't believe the deception but in another replication, Rosenhan (1970) found that 70% said they did believe.

- Milgram said participants were very distressed therefore did believe and afterwards very few said they didn't believe. Sheridan and King (1972) found participants knowingly delivered real shocks to puppies therefore disbelief not an explanation.

- Consider also: *confounding variables* (e.g. use of unknown drug in Hofling *et al.*'s study) and *demand characteristics* (in Asch's study).

KEY DEFINITION

Ecological validity

- One aspect of external validity.

- Being able to generalise findings beyond particular setting of the experiment,

- In order to make statements about real life.

EXAMPLES of low ecological validity in social influence research

- Orne and Holland (1968) claimed Milgram's study tested the experimenter-participant relationship and therefore findings can't be generalized. Milgram said real life is no different. Milgram's findings also replicated in other settings.

- But Mandel (1998) found real life events in Poland during WWII can't be explained by Milgram's studies (page 45).

- Hofling *et al.*'s study was replicated by Rank and Jacobsen who found reverse findings, suggesting low ecological validity (though some important details were changed).

- Trivial tasks: Asch's study and Moscovici's study involved trivial tasks rather than tasks with real life relevance.

⟳ PUTTING IT ALL TOGETHER

Studies that are well-controlled (high internal validity) may not be believable (low internal validity) and may not represent real life (low ecological validity). It is difficult to balance internal validity against external validity and also against ethical considerations.

Cognitive psychology >
Developmental psychology >
Physiological psychology >
Individual differences >
Social psychology >
Research methods >

Conformity and minority influence >
Obedience >
Critical issue: Ethical issues >

Ethical issues
Dealing with ethical issues

KEY DEFINITION

Ethical issues

- Arise where there are conflicting sets of values about the goals, procedures or outcomes of a study.
- Ethical issues are resolved using e.g. ethical guidelines.

KEY DEFINITION

Deception

- Withholding information or misleading participants.
- In order to collect unbiased data.
- Prevents informed consent.

KEY DEFINITION

Informed consent

- Providing comprehensive information concerning the nature and purpose of research and participants' role.
- Participants should be allowed to agree or refuse to participate based on such information.
- Conflict between participants' rights and validity of study.

KEY DEFINITION

Protection of participants from psychological harm

- Participants should be protected from undue psychological risk during an investigation.
- Includes embarrassment, loss of dignity or self-esteem.
- Conflict between participants' rights and researchers' interests.

Other ethical issues

Right to withdraw – Milgram gave participants this right but 'prods' were used.

Confidentiality – Milgram used participants' names.

Invasion of privacy – e.g. Bickman's study.

EXAMPLES of deception in social influence research

- Asch told his participants that the study was about visual perception.
- Milgram told participants it was a study of the effects of punishment on learning.
- Hofling et al. didn't tell the participants that they were involved in a study.

Was the deception necessary? In one study, Gallo et al. (1973) found participants behaved the same whether they were deceived or not.

When is deception acceptable? In memory experiments. Christiansen (1988) found that participants in studies using deception don't object as long as not extreme.

EXAMPLES of lack of informed consent in social influence research

- Gamson et al. offered informed consent of a kind, participants agreed to take part in various studies including one where they would be deceived.
- Zimbardo et al. gave informed consent, but participants did not expect to be arrested at home nor did they fully understand what they had agreed to.

EXAMPLES of psychological harm in social influence research

- Milgram: participants were seen to 'sweat, tremble, stutter, bite their lips'. Three participants reportedly had 'full-blown uncontrollable seizures'.
- Asch: participants may have felt ashamed because appeared to conform so mindlessly.
- Hofling et al.: participants may have been less trustful of doctors, harming professional relationships.
- Darley (1992) suggests that the experience of apparently administering shocks (Milgram's study) may activate a previously dormant aspect of an individual's personality such that they feel more able and more motivated to repeat the actions.

Do participants suffer lasting effects? Milgram's participants were interviewed a year later by a psychiatrist; Zimbardo re-interviewed his participants in the weeks and months after the study and both found no lasting negative effects. Participants claimed to have learned important lessons from the studies.

PUTTING IT ALL TOGETHER

Deception, lack of informed consent and psychological harm were all necessary parts of the design in many social influence studies. It was presumed that participants' rights were not overly abused.

Cognitive psychology >
Developmental psychology >
Physiological psychology >
Individual differences >
Social psychology >
Research methods >

Conformity and minority influence >
Obedience >
Critical issue: Ethical issues >

Ethical issues
Dealing with ethical issues

KEY DEFINITION

KEY DEFINITION

Ethical guidelines

- Concrete, quasi-legal document.

- Produced by professional organization such as the APA or BPS.

- Helps to guide conduct within psychology by establishing principles for standard practice and competence.

How do psychologists deal with ethical issues?

1. **Ethical guidelines** Rules set by a professional organization such as the APA or BPS.

2. **Ethical committees** Group appointed by a research institution to evaluate research proposals.

3. **Socialisation** Learning about ethics as part of studying psychology.

4. **Punishment** Offenders may be barred from their professional organization and working as a psychologist.

5. **Legislation** Research with animals regulated by law (Home Office Act, 1986).

DEALING with deception

- **Debriefing** Inform candidates of true nature of study after it is conducted, and allow them to discuss their feelings.

- **Right to withhold information**

- **Costs and benefits** Deception acceptable if benefits are sufficient. Savin (1973) claimed benefits in Zimbardo's study were not sufficient to justify costs.

EVALUATION

of the use of guidelines

1. It is difficult to predict costs and benefits prior to conducting a study.

2. It is difficult to quantify costs and benefits even after the study.

3. Do you consider costs and benefits in terms of the individual or of society? Research may not harm the individual but findings may lead to biased treatment of the individual's cultural group.

4. The cost-benefit calculation raises as many ethical issues as it is meant to resolve (Baumrind, 1975).

5. Guidelines absolve the researcher of responsibility.

DEALING with informed consent

- **Presumptive consent** Ask for others' opinion and presume participants feel the same. Students questioned by Milgram before his study predicted that no more than 3% of participants would give maximum shocks.

- **Prior general consent** Gamson et al.'s participants agreed to take part in various studies including one where they would be deceived.

DEALING with protection from psychological harm

- **Anticipating harm and stopping study**, e.g. Zimbardo et al. and Gamson et al.

- **Using role play**, e.g. Zimbardo et al. – but still distress experienced.

- **Use of questionnaires** (ask people how they would behave), e.g. Milgram asked students beforehand – but findings completely different.

- **Debriefing**, but may not reduce distress experienced.

PUTTING IT ALL TOGETHER

Milgram, Asch, Zimbardo and others dealt with ethical issues raised in their studies by providing adequate debriefing, arguing for the importance of the research, and in Zimbardo's case stopping the study. Nowadays ethical committees perform an important role in dealing with ethical issues.

Cognitive psychology	>	Quantitative and qualitative research methods	>	**Research methods**
Developmental psychology	>			
Physiological psychology	>	Research design and implementation	>	
Individual differences	>			
Social psychology	>	Data analysis	>	
Research methods	>			

KEY DEFINITION

Research method

A way of conducting research in a systematic manner.

KEY DEFINITION

Quantitative research method

Concerned with measuring 'how much'.

KEY DEFINITION

Qualitative research method

In-depth data is collected reflecting participants' feelings, attitudes and thoughts i.e. data that cannot be directly observed.

	Nature and use	Advantages and weaknesses
Laboratory experiment	IV manipulated to observe effect on DV, controlled conditions.	(+) Can draw causal conclusion. (+) Confounding variables minimized. (+) Can be easily replicated. (−) Artificial, contrived situation. (−) Investigator and participant effects.
Field experiment	Investigate causal relationships in more natural surroundings, IV directly manipulated by experimenter to observe effect on DV.	(+) Usually higher ecological validity than lab. (+) Avoids some participant effects. (−) Less control. (−) More time-consuming.
Natural experiment	IV not directly manipulated, participants not randomly allocated.	(+) Allows research where IV can't be manipulated. (+) Enables psychologists to study 'real' problems. (−) Cannot demonstrate causal relationships. (−) Inevitably many confounding variables.
Investigations using correlational analysis	Co-variables examined for positive, negative or zero association.	(+) Can be used when not possible to manipulate variables. (+) Can rule out a causal relationship. (−) People often misinterpret correlations. (−) There may be other, unknown variables.
Naturalistic observations	Everything left as normal, all variables free to vary.	(+) Study behaviour where can't manipulate variables. (+) High ecological validity. (−) Poor control of extraneous variables. (−) Observer bias, leads to low observer reliability.
Questionnaire surveys	Set of written questions.	(+) A lot of data can be collected. (+) Does not require specialist administrators. (−) Leading questions, *social desirability bias*. (−) Biased samples.
Interviews	Questions can be predetermined, or created in response to answers.	(+) Lots of 'rich' data. (+) Telephone interviews. (−) *Social desirability bias, interviewer bias*. (−) Requires skilled personnel.

Cognitive psychology >	Quantitative and qualitative research methods >	Research designs
Developmental psychology >		Key terms associated with research design
Physiological psychology >	Research design and implementation >	
Individual differences >		Other terms related to research design
Social psychology >	Data analysis >	
Research methods >		

DESIGN of naturalistic observations

Consider:

- Behavioural categories (checklists).

- Sampling techniques (time or event sampling).

- Avoid observer bias, ensure *inter-observer reliability*.

- Ethical issues, e.g. privacy, informed consent.

DESIGN of questionnaire surveys

Consider:

- Writing good questions (issues include: clarity, bias, analysis).

- Kinds of questions (open/closed, fixed choice, Likert scale or semantic differential).

- Writing good questionnaires (sampling, order of questions, use of filler questions, pilot study).

- Ethical issues, e.g. confidentiality.

DESIGN of interviews

Consider:

- Structured, semi-structured (*clinical method*) and unstructured.

- Writing good questions (avoid *social desirability bias*).

- Ethical issues, e.g. confidentiality.

DESIGN of experiments

Repeated measures Same participants in each condition.	(+) Good control for participant variables. (+) Fewer participants. (−) Order effect (e.g. boredom, practice). (−) Participants guess the purpose of the experiment.
Independent groups Two (or more) groups of participants, one for each condition.	(+) Avoids order effects and participants guessing the purpose of the experiment. (−) Needs more participants. (−) Lacks control of participant variables (can use random allocation).
Matched participants (pairs) Participants *matched* on key participant variables.	(+) No order effects. (+) Participant variables partly controlled. (−) Matching is difficult and never totally successful.

Cognitive psychology	>	Quantitative and qualitative research methods	>	Research designs
Developmental psychology	>			Key terms associated with research design
Physiological psychology	>	Research design and implementation	>	
Individual differences	>			Other terms related to research design
Social psychology	>	Data analysis	>	
Research methods	>			

KEY TERMS (terms/concepts specified in the specification which can be used in questions)

Control	Attempts to prevent participants' behaviour being affected by anything other than what was intended. The *independent variable* is intended to have an effect. An *extraneous variable* is one that might have an unintended effect. A *confounding variable* is one that has had an effect on participant's behaviour (i.e. the *dependent variable*). Control of investigator effects may be achieved through *single* or *double blind*, use of *placebos*, *standardised instructions*. Control of *extraneous variables* may be achieved through *random allocation* (of participants to experimental groups), *counterbalancing* (balance order effects), *standardised procedures*.
Demand characteristics	Features of an experiment that a participant, unconsciously, responds to when searching for clues about how to behave. *A confounding variable.*
Dependent variable (DV)	The DV *depends* in some way on the IV.
Directional hypothesis	States which set of scores will be better/faster, positively/negatively correlated. Used when previous research has suggested a direction.
Ethics	Ethical issues arise where there are conflicting values concerning the goals, procedures or outcomes of research. These are dealt with e.g. using guidelines, ethical committees, socialization, prior general consent.
Experimental/alternative hypothesis	A statement of the relationship between the IV and DV. An alternative to the *null hypothesis*. Previous research suggests the direction.
Hypothesis	A clear statement, made at the beginning of an investigation, that aims to predict or explain events.
Independent variable (IV)	Manipulated by the experimenter in order to observe effects on *dependent variable*.
Investigator effects	Anything the investigator does which has an effect on a participant's performance in a study other than what was intended e.g. *experimenter bias*, *interviewer bias*.
Non-directional hypothesis	States that there will be a difference/relationship but does not state the direction. Used when previous research is contradictory.
Null hypothesis	A statement of no difference or no relationship. Used in order to have a baseline conclusion in a research study.
Operationalisation	Variables stated in a form that can be tested (operations).
Participant reactivity	The fact that participants react to cues in an experimental situation because, for example, they want to please the experimenter.
Pilot study	A small-scale trial run of a study to test the design, with a view to making improvements.
Random sampling	Every member of the *population* has an equal chance of being selected. Place all names of everyone in the research *population* in a hat and draw the required number.
Research aims	The stated intentions of a study, to be clear about the purpose.
Selection of participants (sampling)	A technique used to identify potential participants so that they are representative of a *population* (the group from whom the sample is drawn).

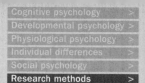

Cognitive psychology >	Quantitative and qualitative research methods >	Research designs
Developmental psychology >		**Key terms associated with research design**
Physiological psychology >	**Research design and implementation >**	
Individual differences >		Other terms related to research design
Social psychology >	Data analysis >	
Research methods >		

KEY TERMS (terms/concepts specified in the specification which can be used in questions)

RELIABILITY

Reliability	The extent to which a measure is consistent.
Improving reliability	Internal reliability: *Test-retest* (give participants same test a second time and compare results), *Split-half method* (divide test items and compare results). External reliability: *Inter-observer reliability* (compare observations made by different observers to check consistency).

VALIDITY

Validity	The legitimacy of a study. If the study has tested what it intended to test it has *internal validity*. If it can be generalized to other settings it has *external validity*. *Experimental validity* refers to the internal and external validity of an experiment.
External (ecological) validity	Ability to generalise to situations beyond the experiment (i.e. to other *people*, other *settings* and over *time*). *Ecological validity* refers to being able to generalise from one setting to another.
Improving validity	Internal validity: reduce *experimenter bias*, *demand characteristics*, control *extraneous variables*. External validity: select representative samples, use realistic settings.
Internal validity	The extent to which a study measures what it claims to measure. Observed effect attributed to experimental manipulation rather than some other factor. Reduced by e.g. *demand characteristics, confounding variables*.

Cognitive psychology >	Quantitative and qualitative research methods >	Research designs
Developmental psychology >		Key terms associated with research design
Physiological psychology >	Research design and implementation >	
Individual differences >		Other terms related to research design
Social psychology >	Data analysis >	
Research methods >		

OTHER TERMS (research concepts not identified in the specification, but that are likely to be useful when answering questions)

Confederate	An ally of the experimenter. Often acts as an IV and therefore an important part of the design.
Control condition	In *repeated measures* design, the condition that provides a baseline measure of behaviour before the IV.
Control group	In *independent groups* design, a group of participants who receive no treatment. Their behaviour acts as a baseline to make comparisons with experimental group.
Counterbalancing	*Order effects* balanced to make sure each condition comes first or second in equal amounts.
Cross-sectional design	An alternative to *longitudinal design*, individuals of different ages compared at same point in time (IV = age).
Debriefing	Post-experimental interview to compensate for any deception, check whether participants did believe in the setup, and elicit feedback from participant about aspects of the study. It is not an ethical issue, it is a means of *dealing* with ethical issues such as deception.
Double blind	The investigator does not know the purpose of the experiment, to prevent expectations influencing the participant's behaviour.
Experimental condition	In *repeated measures* design, the condition containing the IV.
Experimental group	In *independent groups* design, a group of participants who receive the experimental treatment (the IV). An experiment may have more than one experimental group.
Experimenter bias	The effect of an experimenter's expectations, communicated unconsciously, on a participant's behaviour.
Interviewer bias	The effect of an interviewer's expectations on interviewee's behaviour through, for example, leading questions.
Longitudinal design	A study is conducted over a long period of time, to compare the same individual at different points in time (IV = age).
Opportunity sampling	Selecting people who are most easily available. Conducted by asking the first people you encounter in a specific situation.
Order effect	In a *repeated measures* design, a *confounding* variable arising from the order conditions are presented, e.g. a *practice* or *boredom* effect.
Placebo conditions	Control condition where participants think they are receiving the experimental treatment.
Random allocation	Allocating participants to experimental groups randomly. Also randomly allocate items on a test.
Significance	A 'significant result' is one where we can accept the research hypothesis.
Single blind	Use of deception to prevent the participant knowing the purpose of an experiment.
Social desirability bias	The desire to appear favourably.
Standardised instructions	A set of instructions that are the same for all participants. To avoid *investigator effects*.
Standardised procedures	A set of procedures that are the same for all participants. To enable replication.
Volunteer sampling	Participants become part of a study by volunteering. Place an advertisement in a suitable place.

Cognitive psychology >	Quantitative and qualitative research methods >	Data analysis
Developmental psychology >	Research design and implementation >	
Physiological psychology >		
Individual differences >	Data analysis >	
Social psychology >		
Research methods >		

Methods of DATA ANALYSIS

Quantitative analysis	e.g. frequency counts, measures of central tendency and dispersion, bar charts and histograms.	(+) Easy to analyse. (+) Produces neat conclusions. (−) Oversimplifies reality. (−) Experimenter bias, demand characteristics.
Qualitative analysis	e.g. *thematic analysis* (selecting themes beforehand and organizing responses according to the themes) or *grounded theory* (developing themes from the data) or *giving voice* (using participants' own words).	(+) Represents complexity of human behaviour. (+) Provides rich detail. (−) More difficult to detect patterns and reach conclusions. (−) Subjective, affected by personal expectations and beliefs.

Measures of CENTRAL TENDENCY

Mean
Add numbers, divide by number of numbers.
(+) Makes use of all the data.
(−) Misrepresentative if extreme values at one end.

Median
Middle value in an ordered list.
(+) Not affected by extreme scores.
(−) Not as 'sensitive' as the mean.

Mode
The most common value(s).
(+) Useful when the data in categories.
(−) Not useful when there are several modes.

Measures of DISPERSION

Range
Highest to lowest.
(+) Easy to calculate.
(−) Affected by extreme values.

Standard deviation
Mathematical calculation.
(+) Precise, all values taken into account.
(−) Harder to calculate.

The nature of CORRELATIONS

Positive	Co-variables increase together.
Negative	One increases while other decreases.
Zero	No relationship.
Correlation coefficient	A number that tells us how closely the co-variables in a correlational analysis are related.

GRAPHS and CHARTS

Histogram	Graph showing continuous frequency data with a true zero.
Bar charts	Graph showing frequency data; data need not be continuous.
Frequency polygon	Graph showing frequency data, by placing dot at top of each column of a bar chart or histogram and connecting lines.
Scattergraph	For correlations. Scatter of dots. Each dot represents one case.